The UnRules

The UnRules
Man, Machines and the Quest to Master Markets

IGOR TULCHINSKY

WILEY

This edition first published 2018
© 2018 Igor Tulchinsky

Registered office
John Wiley & Sons Ltd, The Atrium, Southern Gate, Chichester, West Sussex, PO19 8SQ, United Kingdom

For details of our global editorial offices, for customer services and for information about how to apply for permission to reuse the copyright material in this book please see our website at www.wiley.com.

Wiley publishes in a variety of print and electronic formats and by print-on-demand. Some material included with standard print versions of this book may not be included in e-books or in print-on-demand. If this book refers to media such as a CD or DVD that is not included in the version you purchased, you may download this material at http://booksupport.wiley.com. For more information about Wiley products, visit www.wiley.com.

Designations used by companies to distinguish their products are often claimed as trademarks. All brand names and product names used in this book are trade names, service marks, trademarks or registered trademarks of their respective owners. The publisher is not associated with any product or vendor mentioned in this book.

Limit of Liability/Disclaimer of Warranty: While the publisher and author have used their best efforts in preparing this book, they make no representations or warranties with respect to the accuracy or completeness of the contents of this book and specifically disclaim any implied warranties of merchantability or fitness for a particular purpose. It is sold on the understanding that the publisher is not engaged in rendering professional services and neither the publisher nor the author shall be liable for damages arising herefrom. If professional advice or other expert assistance is required, the services of a competent professional should be sought.

Library of Congress Cataloging-in-Publication Data

Names: Tulchinsky, Igor, 1966– author.
Title: The unrules : man, machines and the quest to master markets / by Igor Tulchinsky.
Description: Chichester, West Sussex, United Kingdom : John Wiley & Sons, 2018. | Includes index. |
Identifiers: LCCN 2018003403 (print) | LCCN 2018005290 (ebook) | ISBN 9781119372110 (pdf) | ISBN 9781119372127 (epub) | ISBN 9781119372103 (cloth)
Subjects: LCSH: Success in business. | Strategic planning. | Information technology. | Information society. | Tulchinsky, Igor, 1966–
Classification: LCC HF5386 (ebook) | LCC HF5386 .T82865 2018 (print) | DDC 650.1—dc23
LC record available at https://lccn.loc.gov/2018003403

Cover Design: Ed Johnson

Set in 13/15pt and ITC Garamond Std by SPi Global, Chennai, India

Printed simultaneously in the US, Great Britain and Singapore.

V075741_082818

Contents

Foreword

I gor Tulchinsky and I had very different formative experiences. His childhood was constrained by the spiritual oppression of life in the Soviet Union, while mine was enriched by the opportunities available to middle-class kids in 1950s' America. Yet we had much in common: caring parents, a love of reading, and a fascination with math.

As one of today's leading quantitative investors, Igor understands better than most the numbers that underlie dynamic markets. "Markets can be seen as waves," he writes. "They resemble the regular oscillations of a musical instrument." That's a valid observation, although different from the way I came to learn about business and finance. As a college student, I was influenced by the writings of the late Nobel Laureate Gary Becker, and by personal experiences that made me realize how many aspiring entrepreneurs – especially minorities and women – were being denied access to capital.

Igor's approach has relied on rigorous and sophisticated mathematical analysis to identify trading opportunities. This might seem very different from a reliance on theories of human capital – the talent, training, and experiences of people – and the effects of societal trends on business success that I use. But in reality, we both seek to predict the most likely future based on what we observe. Understanding numbers and understanding people can both yield important insights that contribute to financial success. And we concur on several important points that are discussed in this book:

- All markets contain risk, and without risk there are no gains. Careful research can discover the price of risk more accurately.

- Markets also contain psychological traps, such as confusing correlation with causation. If most people are ensnared by these traps, an objective investor who follows the research – like the proverbial one-eyed man in the land of the blind – has an advantage.
- The best investors seek and distill advice from widely diverse sources.
- The study of markets and the study of biology have much in common. Each is a data-driven information science; each uses predictive algorithms in seeking a needle in a haystack of data. As Igor points out, the next great disease breakthrough might be discovered using the same mathematical techniques he uses to analyze financial data.
- Talent is distributed around the world. Genius lives everywhere.

Igor and I both also believe in history's important lessons. A 2010 book about financial markets said that "real estate prices collapsed, credit dried up and house building stopped." That sounds like a description of 2008. But it actually refers to 1792, during the administration of George Washington. More recently, stock markets dropped sharply, banks curtailed lending, and unemployment rose to double digits. Again, that wasn't 2008, it was 1974. Live long enough and you begin to appreciate what remains constant through cycles of history. Yet also note that history isn't a sine wave that repeats patterns exactly; it's more like a helix – similar events return in a different orbit. This is why research is crucial.

Investors who conduct careful research are usually better insulated against inevitable market downturns. They understand that the value of debt securities underpins all capital markets, that leverage is a dangerous tool in volatile markets, that ratings are not always a reliable measure of credit quality, that interest rates are not predictable, and that government actions often distort markets.

Although these basic investing principles change little over time, the tools of finance have changed dramatically. When I studied quantitative economics at Berkeley in the 1960s, computers were expensive, relatively inaccessible, room-sized machines with little power to model investment scenarios. By 1976 processing was speedier, but the storage cost for the IBM System/370 that my business installed was still $1 million per megabyte. Today data processing is millions of times faster, available to nearly anyone on earth, with virtually infinite storage in the cloud at a cost that approaches zero.

This technology revolution has changed the world in many fields. Its impact on biomedical research and precision medicine, for example, has accelerated clinical science and saved untold numbers of lives. There is great opportunity for it to advance beyond its current state through partnerships such as the WorldQuant Initiative for Quantitative Prediction at Weill Cornell, which Igor founded. In the area of finance and investing, Igor and his colleagues now can do what 1960s' finance students could only dream of – simulate reality by creating millions of algorithms (called alphas) that identify trading opportunities with remarkable speed and accuracy.

Although we see markets through different lenses, Igor and I are in complete agreement on one of the most important social issues of our time: providing a path to a meaningful life for every worker, no matter how much traditional work is disrupted by advancing technology. In 2017 we co-authored a *Wall Street Journal* opinion article about the challenges of automation and artificial intelligence. We concluded that digital innovation and robots are opening new possibilities for workers and that the future workplace can provide the opportunity for lives of purpose. We believe, in short, that technology leverages human capital and that wisely deployed technology creates more jobs than it destroys. The key, of course, is to provide abundant opportunities for training and retraining.

The workplace of the future can already be seen in the international operations of Igor's company, WorldQuant. Separately, the WorldQuant Foundation's WorldQuant University offers students a tuition-free online master's degree program in financial engineering. By providing opportunities for a diverse group of bright people who are willing to work hard toward a clear goal, Igor is expanding human capital and helping assure a more prosperous tomorrow. *The UnRules* is a valuable guide for getting there.

Michael Milken
Chairman of the Milken Institute

Preface

People who know me well are aware that I'm a man of few words. In fact, I joke that you only have so many words in life, and when you use them up, you die. Of course, now that I've written this book, I'm living dangerously.

When we are born, our languages are bestowed upon us. I was born in the Soviet Union, in Minsk, now the capital of Belarus, and I grew up speaking Russian. When my parents and I left the Soviet Union and came to the United States, in the late 1970s, we had to master English. As a child, I grasped the new language more easily than my parents did, but – as with the challenging task of adjusting to a strange new culture – we coped. Mathematics was a language I felt comfortable with. I had played chess as a child, and my parents were professional musicians; both pastimes are rooted in a mathematical, rules-based order. Soviet schools excelled at teaching math, and when I was in middle school in Wichita, Kansas, I discovered computer programming. From the start I was drawn to the precision of early computer languages: BASIC and, later, C. When I stumbled into video game development at age 17, I was assigned to co-write a book about video game programming. My experience in early video gaming – coming up with characters (and jokes), writing the programs, working on the book – convinced me that just about anything is possible.

This book, *The UnRules*, is about languages of many kinds: scientific, mathematical, computer, financial, biological. It's about codes, patterns, and signals, and the attempt to extract order from a noisy world. The notion of the UnRule, which lies at the heart of this book, is a kind of philosophy, based on empirical experiences both in financial markets and in life, where no rule, dogma, ideology, paradigm, or model lasts forever and no trading or market relationship performs as you expect all the time. Like a tether on a balloon, the UnRule limits the reach of all the other rules I've gathered over the years. For me, an intense involvement in competitive markets, and in building my career and my quantitative investment firm, WorldQuant, led me to develop rules that apply not just to trading but to life. Many of those rules are rooted in an always uncertain future. This is reflected in my firm's deep involvement in developing alphas – that is, algorithms that seek to predict certain market relationships. The alphas we develop, now numbering in the millions, consist of mathematical expressions and computer code. We rigorously back-test them with historical market data to "simulate" their performance, just as video games simulate different realities. Much of this investment process is extensively automated.

And yet we do not just hand over trading to machines. People matter. Over the years we have learned a lot about alpha design and development. We've learned that no matter how well an alpha is back-tested, it will probably not perform as well when we put it into real markets, and like the rules, no alpha lasts forever. We've learned about the use and dangers of correlation, the management of risk, and the deployment of extraordinary numbers of alphas. We've developed a sense of when to assume risk and, very importantly, when to take losses.

Along these lines, I have found that some life decisions have no clear solutions. For many years I made disciplined but incremental empirical decisions – hiring, for instance, only when I could find genuine talent. There was no master plan. Eventually, we discovered we could find the brightest people in quantitative fields and teach them finance. Smart, motivated people learn quickly. That search for talent transformed WorldQuant into a global firm, exploiting the fact that talent is universal but opportunities are not.

My parents and I had to risk a long journey to America to find the freedom to take advantage of opportunities. Today WorldQuant offers citizens of many nations those same chances, while allowing them to remain at home – in Bulgaria, China, India, Israel, Russia, and Vietnam, among other countries. That recognition that talent requires opportunity also lies behind my recent philanthropic efforts to provide free online education in quantitative disciplines through WorldQuant University, a not-for-profit entity legally separate from the firm.

Today we find ourselves in exciting scientific and technological waters. The drive of any investment firm is to try to predict the path of a market's complex turbulence, which we have labored to decipher and define through alphas. But prediction is never easy. There is an unresolved tension captured by the UnRule. We have been riding great leaps in computer power and an explosion of data of all kinds. We have only just begun to explore this new world, which has amazing possibilities and profound challenges.

The UnRules ends with that curve of exponential growth in alphas bending toward the sky. In WorldQuant we have built a company uniquely suited to this dawning age of broad exponential growth. *The UnRules* is not a long book, but I hope it conveys a sense of the ceaseless searching and testing and experimentation that occur at a firm like WorldQuant. In fact, this book is about beginnings rather than endings. I'm still not a believer in using too many words, but there will be more to say as we explore this new world in more profound ways.

Many books have deep roots. *The UnRules* goes back to my childhood, listening to my parents practice their music every day in our apartment in Minsk. Authors often thank their parents; none of us would be here without them. But mine embodied many of the virtues that found their way into my rules: hard work, persistence, discipline, goal-setting, the willingness to take a risk to reach a valuable end, all bound together by love. And without Millennium Management's Izzy Englander, WorldQuant would not exist. He has been my boss, my mentor, and my friend for many years.

Parts of this book were first composed in an internal publication for the WorldQuant community in 2013. Wendy Goldman Rohm, my literary agent, was instrumental in conceptualizing aspects of the book and finding a publisher. Weill Cornell Medicine's

Dr. Christopher Mason, the subject of Chapter 9, has entertained and enlightened me in conversation for a number of years, and kindly made sure I got my biology right. Several WorldQuant colleagues read parts or all of this book in draft, offering comments and suggestions, pointing out errors, refreshing memories. They include Scott Bender, Jeffrey Blomberg, Anuraag Gutgutia, Richard Hu, Geoffrey Lauprete, Nitish Maini, and Paradorn Pasuthip. And ably overseeing and managing the editorial process was WorldQuant's global head of content, Michael Peltz. Finally, I'd like to acknowledge all my many colleagues at WorldQuant over the years. This book, and our success, would not be possible without your faith and support.

Igor Tulchinsky
December 2017

CHAPTER 1

Quake

"Take aggressive risks, but manage losses."

On the morning of August 6, 2007, a Monday, I arrived early at WorldQuant's office in Old Greenwich, Connecticut. I had a lot on my mind: I was in the middle of moving, my head filled with the logistical details of movers, schedules, and the kids. By 10 a.m., however, I knew something was wrong. We had been hit, seemingly out of nowhere, by a wave of losses on our statistical-arbitrage trades – a strategy, common to a hedge fund firm like WorldQuant, that takes advantage of pricing differentials between related financial securities.

As the hours ticked by, anxiety quietly gripped the office. Because our trading is automated, the atmosphere at a quantitative investment management firm like WorldQuant resembles a library far more than it does a frantic trading floor. Nobody's screaming or rushing around. But that Monday you could feel the tension. There was little laughter, and the portfolio managers, clearly nervous, drifted in to discuss their exposures. The next day it got worse.

WorldQuant had been in existence for only six months, although I had been engaged in quantitative trading, which involves using sophisticated math and large amounts of data to identify trading opportunities, since 1995. At WorldQuant we had poured resources into developing about a hundred predictive algorithms we call alphas: mathematical expressions and computer source code that we rigorously back-test before putting them into production in live investment strategies. All that effort went into ensuring that we *wouldn't* take a hit like the one we were suffering. We knew that individual alphas regularly weaken or fail, and we were no strangers to drawdowns – we experienced significant declines roughly once a year back then. But our alphas were not supposed to fail collectively. This was bad.

You know what they say: When the CEO moves into a new house, it's a signal to sell. What we didn't know immediately was that similar losses were hitting our competitors at other quant firms. Renaissance Technologies, D.E. Shaw, AQR, and Highbridge Capital Management all saw their finely honed strategies take a sudden nosedive. Goldman Sachs, which at the time had one of the largest quant books – $165 billion – eventually lost more than 30%. Just like us, our rivals must have been struggling to figure out what had happened and why it seemed to be happening just to quant firms.

There had been some ominous signs in the surrounding financial world. For much of the summer, fallout from the unfolding subprime mortgage crisis had been sending shock waves through the markets. Bear Stearns was forced to close two mortgage-backed credit funds, and there were signs that European banks were growing wary of lending to one another. But our investment strategies were designed to be market neutral – that is, uncorrelated with the broader market. Those subprime issues, in theory, should not have affected the quantitative strategies we employed at WorldQuant. But then, nearly every quant shop probably thought the same way.

Quant firms are only a slice of the hedge fund world, which in turn is only part of the investing universe. Though firms like WorldQuant were hit hard on August 6, 2007, there were no signs of a broader collapse. The next day the Federal Reserve decided to leave interest rates unchanged. Stocks fell after the announcement, then recovered; that week the S&P 500 edged down only very slightly.

As we tried to figure out what had happened, all we really knew was that our relative-value and statistical-arbitrage alphas were not working, as if their plugs had been pulled. We suspected that someone out there had taken a hit and was liquidating, setting off a chain reaction of selling, but we lacked the time, the distance, and the data to comprehend fully what was going on. We watched nervously as the problem spread from the U.S. to Japan.

Over my trading career I'd learned a number of lessons that had served me well: *Don't get emotional about your trades. React instantly to bad news. If it's scary, run. Take aggressive risks, but manage losses.* Back in August 1998, when I was just building my trading portfolio, the Russian government suddenly devalued the ruble and defaulted on its debt. In the resulting violent drawdown, I saw my entire year's gains evaporate in a few days. A month after that, hedge fund firm Long-Term Capital Management needed a bailout by major banks to avoid causing damage to the American financial system. Now, almost nine years to the day later, that chaotic time was on my mind.

The problem of looking ahead, of course, is that you can't know how big or how long the declines will be. After the first losses on Monday, I made the decision to start liquidating the entire portfolio on Tuesday, giving up all the year-to-date profits. Some of this was my memory of the Russian default, when I held on too long, and some was intuition – observing the fear in people's eyes. Liquidating was difficult to swallow, but on Wednesday the carnage deepened, and we felt lucky to be out of it. On Thursday I came into the office early and made a decision to jump back in with 50% of our capital. I was aware that the market could sweep lower, but once again I was relying on intuition – not just on instinct, but on instinct shaped by experience.

In fact, the markets righted themselves as suddenly as they had declined. Just like that, most of the participants were making money again, though we took a few months to get back to 100% invested. We ended up having a pretty solid year. But those who hesitated to sell, had trouble liquidating, or sold into the recovery doubled their pain.

That August 2007 episode became known as "the quant quake," and it contained a number of lessons: There are risks that you've never thought about, and there are uncertainties. Sometimes you have to act quickly with too few data points. At WorldQuant we may practice quantitative trading, but we also know when to rely on intuition born of experience.

The firm went on to generate stable returns again, and as we accumulated the alphas that we use to build strategies, we experienced fewer significant drawdowns. In the industry the quant quake triggered a rethinking of investment models and a considerable amount of debate. Were too many quantitative hedge funds chasing the same strategies and eliminating the profits? What *did* happen in early August 2007?

To this day the evidence remains circumstantial and no one really knows for sure what set off the quake. But in the subsequent years, we've developed a better idea thanks to academic research. A month or so after the quake, two finance academics, MIT's Andrew Lo and Amir Khandani, tried to unravel what had happened by building quant portfolios and simulating the episode – in a sense, running the history backward. They concluded that somewhere in the markets a large player – Lo and Khandani thought it was a bank, but Bob Litterman, who ran Goldman's quant fund at the time, later argued it was a multistrategy hedge fund – may have taken a hit and quickly sold a large relative-value position to respond to credit-related margin calls or to take risk-reduction measures. Given what was going on at the time, there may have been a link to the growing subprime mortgage problem. Liquidating positions in turn put pressure on quant firms with similar positions heavily invested in equities, made worse by leverage, which magnifies gains in rising markets and losses in falling ones.

Then a contagion effect developed, with the stress in one part of the market spreading to others. Prices fell, and the more they fell, the worse it got. The fact that the quant quake seemed to target relative-value trades may have been a coincidence, but it did suggest that unrelated markets had inadvertently grown more correlated, creating a so-called crowded trade without realizing it, and raising the risk for everyone.

We would see far broader and more dangerous correlations emerge when the global financial crisis broke upon us all. When Lehman Brothers collapsed in September 2008, WorldQuant had another scare: Lehman was our prime broker in Asia and Europe, and its failure meant we couldn't trade our overseas portfolios for several days. But in this case, at least, we knew what the problem was. We quickly negotiated a new prime brokerage relationship and got back into the market in about a week.

As the world struggled to recover from the financial crisis, WorldQuant continued to perform and grow. Today we believe our greatest growth is still ahead of us. We have seen remarkable increases in people and data, computing power and market experience. In fact, it has become clear to me that we are part of an *exponential* revolution in quantitative finance.

What does that mean? I believe that nearly all aspects of WorldQuant's business, and perhaps our broader business lives, are undergoing not linear but exponential growth. As a result, goals that seem shocking today will look normal tomorrow and useless the day after. Exponential thinking requires audacity, not complacency. It means not believing in limits, which are temporary and meant to be broken. It calls for risk-taking as a way of life. In exponential thinking the terrain ahead is always unknown. In unknown terrain there are always bumps; it's a world of turbulence and risk. And the rewards are growing exponentially for those who can digest all this information.

When WorldQuant launched, in 2007, we had 37 employees. Today we employ more than 600 researchers, portfolio managers, technologists, and support staff in 25-plus offices around the world, including over 125 Ph.D.s. Though the number of alphas at our command seemed large in 2007 – and it was, relatively speaking – it has since exploded. We now have more than 10 million alphas archived in the WorldQuant databases, and over the short term our goal is 100 million in the next few years and 1 billion in five to 10 years. That's big, exponential growth, which we expect to happen.

We have built WorldQuant around a handful of core ideas.

Alphas, like ideas, are infinite. Trading can be taught. We believe we hold the future of trading in our hands. We believe that talent is statistically distributed globally but opportunity is not, so we must go out and try to match talent to opportunity. The competitive demands of the market drive us to reach out and continually seek a diversity of opinion – and of ideas, which produce alphas. That's one of the lessons of the quant quake: Don't get sucked into a crowded trade. Think differently.

This means three things. First, WorldQuant is, in part, a technology company that must operate globally to tap talent. Second, WorldQuant is a global *alpha factory*, whose output is an ever-growing stream of diverse investment ideas. Last, WorldQuant must shape itself by exponential thinking – by thinking big. Our view is that with great success comes great responsibility. And some of that sense of responsibility extends to educational efforts, particularly in quantitative fields.

Among the most important responsibilities is translating these core beliefs into concrete actions, finding ways to use WorldQuant's insights and resources to provide people around the world with opportunities to develop and demonstrate their talents.

In 2014 we launched the WorldQuant Challenge, inviting participants to build high-quality alphas. It's part competition, part learning opportunity – contestants use and experiment with our proprietary simulation and back-testing software, WebSim. Just as impressive as the alphas we've seen generated have been the locations from which they were generated. We've had participants hailing from the eastern coast of India to rural China, reinforcing the fact that a few major cities, or even a few countries, don't have a monopoly on talent or great investment ideas.

In 2009 we started the WorldQuant Foundation, which furthers charitable initiatives, including making high-quality education more accessible worldwide, through targeted donations to organizations and helping students continue their journey in education. To date, we've offered scholarships to talented individuals who have graduated from esteemed universities in China, the Middle East, and the U.S.

It struck me that we use technology at WorldQuant to scale our business – why couldn't we use technology to "scale" high-quality education, making it more readily available for students around the world? I wanted to start with a subject that I knew well: quantitative finance. That's why in 2015 we launched WorldQuant University, which offers a free, online master's degree in financial engineering. Two years into the program, we now have about 1,800 students in more than 90 countries. To be clear, the goal of WorldQuant University is to make high-quality education more accessible, not to be a recruiting tool. Therefore, as part of our nonprofit mission, we have agreed not to hire any WorldQuant University graduates for at least a full year after their graduation. Instead, the goal of WorldQuant University is to enable students to become leaders in their communities and fields, further spurring community and industry development.

Underpinning each of these initiatives is my belief in the power of education, in the ability of learning and technology to open the door of opportunity for talented, motivated individuals around the world.

This book brings together aspects of my life, work, and thought. It's part memoir; part my thoughts on markets, math, and science; and part my reflection on what has and hasn't worked in my life and my profession. It's about the development of powerful computing tools and my discovery of computer programming and computer simulation, initially in video games. It's about the interaction of machines, data, and humans. Not surprisingly, a major preoccupation is the nature of financial markets: complex, self-organizing systems that are as natural as the weather, waves, earthquakes, evolution, and deep structures of physics, biology, and math. Prediction is difficult in these complex systems, and disasters always seem to come as a surprise. Quantitative investing is shaped by probability, randomness, correlation, and the law of large numbers.

Two underlying themes provide the focus for *The UnRules*. First, there is the notion of rules – and the central, paradoxical UnRule that no rule or model or alpha is perfect or will survive forever in an ever-changing world. This UnRule is a reality of the trading markets that also applies to life. Some rules will fade as conditions change. Some will prove less effective as a result of their success. Others will recognize their potency and rush to copy them – a phenomenon known as arbitrage. An alpha is a kind of rule, or at least a hypothesis, usually about some relation in the market that will affect securities, a signal amid the market noise. (We will explore these algorithms, which connect man to machine, much more deeply in this book.) As a guide to life and trading, these rules reflect both the universe my colleagues and I created at WorldQuant, with its quantitative strategy, powerful simulation software, and global development of alphas, and the lessons of my own journey from Soviet servitude to American freedom.

.I am often asked how I came to start WorldQuant. Every society, in every age, has placed a high premium on success and money. For some, of course, the goal is frankly material. For others, material goods are a means to other ends: not personal property or a giant bank account, but the ability to pursue goals free of material want, to secure the well-being of those they love and those who depend upon them, confident that their property will not be stolen by thieves or capriciously expropriated by those in power. The freedom to pursue a wide range of goals is part of what allows a society to call itself free – along with the understanding that people differ in what they wish for out of life.

Countless books, courses, and self-help programs promise the accumulation of wealth. I've looked into any number of them. My conclusion? Wealth results from a clearly understood goal and a set of personality traits more than from any particular set of abilities or tricks.

Almost no one begins life with a clear set of goals. Nearly everyone stumbles upon them – some sooner, some later, some never. Goals evolve, shaped by experience and hammered into place by an individual's response to challenge and change. I have had about 30 jobs in my life, and I've lived in about 30 places. My journey has been far from glamorous, and it's left a deep imprint on my psyche. Looking back, I can see how my early life in what then was the Soviet Union, my family's determination to seek freedom, and the jobs I took to help them and support myself all laid the foundation for what came later – and in particular for WorldQuant. Those experiences also left me committed to the values that now guide my life: hard work; persistence; respect for others; uncompromising ethics; gratitude; and the desire for love, family, success, and, especially, self-determination.

That journey began in Minsk.

CHAPTER 2

The UnRule that Rules the Rest

"All theories and all methods have flaws."

I was born in Minsk in 1966. Today Minsk is the capital of Belarus, a landlocked nation with Poland to the west, Ukraine to the south, Lithuania and Latvia to the north, and Russia to the east. But in my youth Belarus was part of the Soviet Union.

I had a large family on both sides, most of them in Leningrad and Minsk. My paternal grandparents had lived in Poland, then fled to the Soviet Union when the Germans attacked. They fled again when the Germans destroyed a large part of Minsk. My grandmother traveled alone to Siberia, where my father was born. My parents were, and are, musicians: My father, Alexander, plays the viola, and my mother, Rimma, is a pianist. They both taught at a prestigious musical school for gifted children that is affiliated with the Belarusian State Conservatory. I grew up listening to my father practice for hours every day. Even though they lacked high connections, my parents had good jobs in the Soviet Union. We had an apartment and a car, and the two of them were able to do what they loved.

My memories of Minsk are scattered: the city wrapped around the Svislach and Nyamiha rivers, the immense GUM department store, and the eternal flame at the base of the obelisk in Victory Square that commemorated the Great Patriotic War – World War II, in which Belarus had suffered disproportionately among the Soviet republics. I remember our big apartment building, and I remember playing with my friends outside. After a while my mother would stick her head out the window and yell my name really, really loud to call me home. If I was anywhere within half a mile, I would race home. I didn't want to make her mad.

Looking back now at the post-Stalinist era, I would say that the Soviets may not have been the worst of overseers. Still, they were undoubtedly overseers. Even those Belarusians who brought much-desired prestige and international renown to the regime, and to the USSR, were only better-paid slaves. To live under the Soviet system without freedom was a terrible spiritual oppression that eroded an individual's inner self slowly, subtly, relentlessly. In the 1970s and 1980s, many people – even the most materially privileged, but especially artists and scientists, including many Jews, like my own family – longed to leave, at whatever the cost. Jews had few opportunities, and there was a degree of anti-Semitism at the time that was evident even to me: Kids would write "Yid" on the sidewalk with chalk without knowing what it meant. After five years of discussing it, my father applied for us to depart the USSR in the winter of 1977. The decision was based on secondhand information trickling back from emigrants who had already left and from shortwave reception of Voice of America. (Today I collect shortwave radios.) This was a difficult decision. Though my parents were accomplished musicians, they were not in the public eye. That reduced the risk of retaliation, but they knew that when they applied to emigrate, the Soviets would fire them from their jobs and keep them from working. The Soviet bureaucrats wanted not merely to make life difficult for "traitors" but to silence them.

My father knew exactly what was at stake, for himself and my mother as people devoted to music; for us as a family; and for me as their only child. My parents were branded "traitors," a term that did not simply convey disapproval but had potentially dreadful consequences in the Soviet Union. Once we declared we were leaving, our friends were afraid to communicate with us. We had to wait for permission from a broad range of authorities, which sometimes never came. At that time, the term "refusenik" attached itself to those who had sought to leave but had been denied by the state, leaving them worse off, isolated and shunned. The emigration process was slow. Though my parents had taken care to save up before announcing their decision, money eventually grew tight.

The Soviet Union had come under great international pressure to allow people to leave. Exit was an option only because of the Jackson–Vanik amendment, which the U.S. Congress had passed in 1974. The USSR had agreed to let some people depart because it wanted to avoid being branded a human rights abuser and losing much-needed most-favored-nation trading status with the U.S. This was a telltale sign of the strain in the crumbling Soviet economy, which over time would lead to the collapse of Soviet communism and the breakup of the Soviet empire.

The international pressure on the Soviet Union stemmed from the heroic resistance of three men: Russian literary giant Alexander

Solzhenitsyn, physicist and Nobel Prize winner Andrei Sakharov, and Sakharov's protégé, chess prodigy and applied mathematician Natan Sharansky.

In *The Gulag Archipelago*, Solzhenitsyn exposed the Soviet Union's chain of prisons in its northern and western tundra. The writer himself had served time in the gulag. His book on the prison system was published in the West in 1973; the next year the Soviet Union expelled him to West Germany. After that Solzhenitsyn traveled to Switzerland and moved to the United States. Sakharov, a major figure in the Soviet development of the hydrogen bomb, turned to activism in the 1960s but was left untouched until 1980, when he was arrested and exiled to Gorky (now Nizhny Novgorod), a city off limits to foreigners. Sharansky was even less lucky. Because chess was very popular in the Soviet Union – an abstract game that, like math, was remote from the state – Sharansky believed the authorities would not dare to send him to the gulag. When he attempted to emigrate to Israel, however, he was blocked. In 1977, the year my father applied to leave the USSR, Sharansky was arrested on charges of spying for the United States, accused of passing along the names of 1,300 refuseniks to the West. He ended up being sentenced to 13 years of solitary confinement and forced labor in a remote camp known as Perm 35, where he famously retained his sanity by playing mental games of chess with himself. Sharansky was freed after nine years and came to the West in a prisoner exchange early in the Mikhail Gorbachev era. He ended up reunited with his family in Israel, where he became a prominent politician and cabinet minister.

When my family lived in Minsk, the only official way out of the Soviet Union was to apply for an invitation from Israel. That wasn't easy – you needed connections – but my parents somehow succeeded. Once out of the Soviet Union, however, they decided to travel to the United States. We were forbidden to take money or assets of any size out of the USSR. So in the summer of 1977, when I was 10, we departed for Poland, each carrying one suitcase, one gold ring, and one camera, most of which we would sell along the way. My parents managed to sneak out a single ruble, which we used to buy chewing gum in Poland. Chewing gum was not available in the Soviet Union and was considered a delicacy. When it melted in my mouth, I spat it out.

We were supported in our move out of the USSR by the Hebrew Immigrant Aid Society (HIAS), a group formed in New York City in the 1880s. My parents were able to keep the worst of our financial situation from me. We didn't stay in Poland long before traveling to Austria, which seemed extremely clean and orderly by comparison. Food was suddenly abundant, and my belly swelled. Then we struck south for Italy. For several months we lived in Rome, in the home of a shoemaker who would stop hammering nails so my father could practice his viola to prepare for finding work in America. My pregnant aunt had come with us; she delivered her baby in Rome. I remember rocking the baby with one hand and holding a book in the other. Waiting for word from the American immigration authorities, my family and I studied English, struggling with the unfamiliar alphabet and pronunciations. As time dragged on, my parents sold our belongings to supplement the funds from the HIAS.

After three long months, word arrived: The Tulchinsky family would be allowed to travel to New York.

Looking back, I can see how my early life and my family's determination to live in freedom laid much of the foundation for what came later. My memories of our travels from the Soviet Union to the U.S. are spotty. Maybe that was my way of coping with the tension and anxiety. Although we'd taken some English classes in Rome, we really learned the language only after we arrived in New York. I picked up English more readily than my parents did. I was still young and I craved learning. I enjoyed reading, I was adept at mathematics, and I was consumed by chess. Unlike my musically gifted parents, I did not play an instrument, but since Pythagoras there's been the recognition that there is a fundamental relation between math and music – the music of the spheres – and, of course, between math and chess.

I was shaped by the experience of leaving Minsk and by the challenges I encountered in America. Not only did I have to break through obstacles and accumulate experience, I had to deliberately learn as much as I could from each effort. Some lessons came as surprises. Others I knew of but had passed over in youthful ignorance until I faced them directly. With time I came to understand that although we must live life to become good at it, we can see our experiences through the eyes of others and learn from them.

In a sense, these lessons, or rules, resemble the alphas we construct and test and trade at WorldQuant. Often they are very faint signals from a noisy reality that we cannot comprehend in its entirety. These signals form patterns that are both empirical and hypothetical, the residue of experience. We can try to define them, to embody them in rules, but even if we succeed, that does not make them infallible, eternal truths. For every rule (or alpha), there may come a time, as in the quant quake of 2007, when they no longer are effective.

What are these rules? Some are broad, almost philosophical.

> *You only live once.* Your time on earth is the only truly irreplaceable resource. You can always make another dollar, but you can never make another minute. You should view your life through the prism of the old question, "If today were my last day, what would I be doing with it?"
>
> *Life is unpredictable.* There are limits to planning; the key is to act. Create the dots and connect them later, because you don't know which dots will materialize. By fostering opportunities, then taking advantage of outcomes, you maximize success. Other rules feed off that.
>
> *Establish only concrete, quantifiable goals, and always go from A to B.* Concrete things are attainable. Abstract and nebulous wishes are not. If you don't have specific goals, your movement through life will be a Brownian motion – random.
>
> *Develop willpower and play to your strengths.* And, importantly, *persist*. Keep at it. Work the problem. Over time, persistence trumps ability.

I have learned many of these lessons from trading, which is life lived at an intense pitch. A number of my rules had to be applied during the quant quake, particularly in dealing with losses. A lot of these rules apply to the quantitative approach we've pioneered at WorldQuant.

Obstacles are information. If you can't get something to work, there's a reason. Maybe it's a bad idea. Maybe you are misinformed. Maybe your actions are inappropriate. Learn, adjust, and attack it again.

Aim for the anxious edge. Make everyone benefit. Opportunity is unlimited. You can always find ways to do better and succeed, in any circumstance, in any business or economic climate. Especially in the stock market, as in science, opportunity is always there because ...

... ideas are infinite. Knowledge grows from knowledge, and good ideas constitute new knowledge, which alters reality as it grows.

Arrogance distorts reality.

All of these rules, however, are subordinated to a paradoxical master rule, the UnRule, which prevails in both markets and in life: *All theories and all methods have flaws. Nothing can be proved with absolute certainty, but anything may be disproved, and nothing that can be articulated can be perfect.* This rule is rooted in the constant necessity to change, to be flexible, to take losses, to always move on, to get your ego out of the way. It represents a flight from fixed and rigid ideas, from dogmas and ideologies.

Like many paradoxes, this UnRule is a bit of a philosophical puzzler. In some ways it's related to the ancient Epimenides paradox, or liar paradox, which is attributed to a sixth-century BC Cretan. This logical paradox involves two statements: One, all Cretans are liars; two, I am a Cretan. Taken together, the two statements create a contradiction – how can a liar tell the truth? In the 1930s, Austrian mathematician Kurt Gödel famously used an aspect of the liar paradox in his first incompleteness theorem, which established inherent limitations to every axiom, or rule, containing basic arithmetic. Simply put, Gödel suggested that at a fundamental level, arithmetic could not be proved and was not truly consistent. In asserting this, Gödel overturned an attempt by Germany's greatest mathematician at that time, David Hilbert, and Britain's Alfred North

Whitehead and Bertrand Russell, to do just that. In any case, my UnRule resembles the liar paradox: All rules are flawed except the rule that declares all rules flawed.

But let's not engage with deep mathematical logic here. The UnRule is an empirical rule. Man is a creature who became successful because of his ability to make sense of his environment and apply rules, from hunting to agriculture to quantum physics. But there are an infinite number of rules that describe reality, and we are always striving to discover more. As Karl Popper, the Vienna-born philosopher of science and proponent of "the open society," argued, it's impossible to verify a universal truth; any future counter-instance could disprove it. Popper stressed that because pure facts don't exist, all observations and the rules developed from observation are subjective and theoretical. Reality is complicated. People and ideas are imperfect. Ideas are expressed as abstractions, in words and symbols. Rules are just metaphorical attempts to capture an elusive reality. Thus, every single rule is flawed and no rule works all the time. No single dogma describes the world. But many rules describe the world a little bit.

Again, I suppose I developed some of this worldview because of my experience: the flight from Russia, the struggle to adjust to a new world. That experience, I think, has put a premium on searching for the rules of the game at hand, but adjusting when things go awry – cutting losses, which is a practical application of the UnRule.

The UnRule also opens the door to a variety of subjects that have long fascinated me because they offer glimpses into the complexities of nature and man: mathematics, computer programming and simulation, the interaction of man and machine, the nature of markets and other complex, self-organizing systems.

My immersion in these large and fascinating subjects began after my family arrived in New York in late 1978.

CHAPTER 3

Parallel Universes

"Events don't unfold as anticipated, so there are limits to what can be planned."

The Greystone Hotel, at West 91st Street and Broadway on Manhattan's Upper West Side, was home to vermin of every kind. And it was home to us, temporarily. We had checked into the rundown hotel on a word-of-mouth recommendation. That's how things worked in the immigrant community. The Upper West Side was for us what the Lower East Side had been for Jews fleeing Europe seven decades earlier.

In those days the neighborhood was a bustling, if declining and crime-ridden, part of Manhattan. The hotel, erected in the 1920s, fit right in. I would amuse myself watching American cockroaches race in and out of their hideaways as *Tom and Jerry* played on the television. It was harder to adapt to some aspects of our new life: The local food, which was highly processed and packed with preservatives, made me sick, unlike European food. But even then, in the late 1970s, change was churning beneath the Upper West Side's shabby surface. Twenty years later I would live across the street from the Greystone in what was then a gentrifying part of New York; my first child was born there. Today the Greystone offers luxury apartments aimed at the young and affluent, and features a gym and a rooftop garden.

My family struggled in New York. It didn't matter that my parents had been accomplished musicians in the Soviet Union. In their new home they were immigrants, just another Russian family in a sea of newcomers. Chat with a Manhattan cabbie today, and often you will find a representative of the same uncomplaining group, simply glad to be able to make a living. Today that cabbie might be an engineer from Afghanistan or a physician from Iraq; a generation ago he was a Buddhist from Vietnam or a Russian Jew. None of them, including my parents, considered themselves "poor." They were free, that's what mattered. Their children would rise in America, and that's what counted.

Even though we were foreigners in America, New York was a natural destination for us. There was a large and diverse Russian community in Brooklyn's Brighton Beach, near Coney Island. Most important, Manhattan was the country's center of culture, the humanities, and art, to which my parents had devoted their

professional lives. Our hotel may have been dingy, but 25 blocks to
the north was Columbia University and 25 blocks south was Lincoln
Center and the Juilliard School.

My mother found a series of low-paying jobs – her main con-
cern was being home with me – and my father took whatever
musical gigs he could get in a city overflowing with musicians.
Anyone who is a professional classical musician knows that well-
paying, single-shot engagements are rare; a position that provides a
living wage with security is even harder to find. My father practiced
every day, and he was good, but in New York 400 to 500 people
would turn up at auditions for even the smallest musical job. This
put a great deal of pressure on my father, who had a family to
support and spoke limited English. He had little time to do anything but audition.

In my first few months in New York, I didn't venture very far
from the Greystone. Because it was summer, I didn't go to school,
so I couldn't pick up much English. In the fall my parents put me
into the neighborhood public school. In Russia I had been in the
fourth grade, but in America I qualified for the sixth. The schools
in Minsk taught more math than their American counterparts, but
American schools taught many other things. I began to pick up
English very quickly. I'd take my homework and a dictionary and
look up words I didn't know.

I'd only been in my Manhattan school for a few weeks when
my family moved to Astoria, Queens. There my school was not that
nice. It was a tough neighborhood and a bit of a shock.

In less than a year, my father found a steady position with the
Richmond Symphony, and we headed south to Virginia. My father
had to learn a lot of the symphonic parts because he'd been teaching
for so many years. In some ways Richmond was as big a change for
me as New York had been. For one thing, we lived in the suburbs.
After two years we moved again, this time to Wichita, Kansas.

To a New Yorker, Wichita was *Gunsmoke* country, but the city
actually had a long cultural history and a fine symphony orchestra.
The cost of living was much lower there than in New York, and my
father found work – just not enough of it.

My parents never complained. They were grateful and fulfilled in their new life, and they took pride in the fact that they could shield me from the difficulties they faced. That's not to say I had it easy. I learned a great deal about making my way through life in those years. And although my parents protected me, they refused to coddle me. My father encouraged me to find work, and I did, at age 13: I was paid 10 cents an index card to create a card catalogue for a personal library consisting of several thousand books and magazines. I was very conscientious, but I was young, and boredom soon settled in.

I had a lot of jobs in those early years. One summer I worked as a dishwasher in a Wichita steakhouse. The temperature in the kitchen was in the 90s, and the floor was covered with a thin film of grease, so you could – and you almost had to – skate from place to place as you worked. That job paid $3.35 an hour. Dishwashing was neither fun nor visibly enriching, but it taught me persistence and the importance of being willing to take on unglamorous but necessary tasks. I left that job, however, for a position paying a slightly higher wage, $3.45, at a bakery across the street. I made cookies and sandwiches well into the next morning.

I learned a lot in Wichita, but the most important thing I learned in those years was computer programming. My high school had a handful of Apple IIe machines, and I was hooked immediately. I can still see and feel the keyboard. My introduction to programming was an educational language developed in the late 1960s called Logo. Former child hackers may fondly recall the robotic turtle (later an on-screen turtle-like cursor) used to input commands in Logo. It was a full-scale programming language that introduced children to the power of computing, offering more than prepackaged applications.

While still in high school, I got a job teaching Logo at a camp for physically handicapped adults. But on the first day, the teacher failed to show and I had to deal with the class myself. It was a memorable experience. Many of my students were severely limited, but having computer access allowed them to express themselves in exciting new ways. I learned a lot about them – and about myself.

I realized how smart and capable people could be when given the chance and the proper tools. And I saw that any situation could be managed when circumstances forced me to perform. If the teacher didn't show up, I could teach the class, and do pretty much anything else I might be called upon to do, with or without formal training.

Next I taught myself a more powerful programming language: BASIC. One day a physician from a local hospital came to my high school and asked who could program. The school pointed to me and my computer friend, a German kid. By then we had both mastered BASIC. He hired us to write programs that set antibiotic dosages at the hospital. Although the doctor supervised us, the doses were determined by a BASIC program written by 15-year-olds. We could have killed a hundred people, but our programs worked, and I learned another critical lesson: The most important limit is how much ability and persistence you have. Age means little.

When I was 17, my family moved to Houston. We liked Texas. Once again my father urged me to get a job, directing me to the classified section of our local newspaper. There I spotted an advertisement for a video game programming job that paid $20 an hour, a fortune for a teenager back then. I jumped into our car (I had just learned to drive) and nervously negotiated Houston's tangled traffic to the firm's office. I met the president of the company, who laid out the responsibilities of the programming job in simple terms: "Your mission is this: We give you a name, you write us a video game. How about that?"

"Okay," I said. "No problem."

The names he threw out were interesting: *Death Valley Patrol*, *Sound the Whistle*, *Ghost Hunt*, *Yorick's Revenge*. They were designed to run on the then-new Commodore 64 home computer. So I broke my piggy bank (I actually had one), bought a computer, and began programming. The Commodore 64 was extremely popular in the 1980s, particularly for game developers and players. The language was BASIC, but it was built for speed. Today these games seem very, well, basic – you can still find some of them on YouTube – but the company liked them. I often included funny and morbid elements, like vultures descending from the sky to eat fallen players. Soon I was asked to contribute to a book on video game design, explaining the coding and thinking process behind the games I'd worked on. The book didn't sell many copies, but five of my games were published.

∾

What I didn't realize as a teenager in Houston was that by stumbling into the video game business I would be swept along by a trend that would powerfully grow in the years ahead: computer simulation. Even in the early days of programming – say, when I was working on *Death Valley Patrol* – I was engaged in building a kind of mirror world, or simulation. By today's standards the programming tools were crude and the computer processing and memory were skimpy. But in every game we were producing new worlds – simulacra.

Simulation, driven by vast amounts of data and faster, more powerful computers, has developed in remarkable ways since my stint as a game programmer. It's now a key tool in the scientific and technological kit bag, and used in many disciplines: in medicine, and self-driving cars, and space vessels that can land themselves on distant planets, and in entertainment of all kinds, with video games and movies edging ever closer together. Pilots train on simulation systems; at WorldQuant alphas undergo rigorous back-testing, simulating the past with huge amounts of market data. Simulation and Big Data have allowed us to tackle very large, complex systems that heretofore were impenetrable.

Why is the hand that controls Adam Smith's market invisible? Because a complex system like the market is, at least in part, self-organizing – that is, subject to some controlling principle, some deep patterning, despite the appearance of randomness. But because Smith and his successors lacked the mathematics and the computing power to begin to penetrate the complexity of even simple markets, the hand remained "invisible" and, for the most part, unpredictable.

The word "complex" does not just mean "complicated." In science a complex system consists of the interaction of many components that do not seem to obey statistical averaging. Complex systems behave in extraordinary ways, arising from the interaction of a multitude of small-scale "agents," such as traders. These systems typically display abrupt, unannounced, random, or chaotic-seeming changes from one state to another ("phase transitions" or "changes of regime"). The changes are so inexplicable that they look like the whims of capricious gods. Yet these features mark all complex systems as "natural" – earthquakes, population spikes or extinctions, weather, climate, volcanism, market or economic booms and busts. They are very difficult to predict, whether they're hurricanes and mudslides or sudden economic slumps like the Great Depression and the global financial crisis. These phenomena can be explained – although the underlying factors are often complex – but very few can predict them with accuracy.

Complex systems' resistance to prediction was a daunting impediment to scientists engaged in building a nuclear bomb during World War II. Part of the credit for the Manhattan Project's eventual success can be given to the development of electronic computers that were primitive by today's standards but still able to make massive calculations. Of course, human genius was an essential accompaniment to that new tool.

In large part that genius was provided by a mathematician, John (Johnny) von Neumann, who left Hungary in the early 1930s for Princeton University's new Institute for Advanced Study (IAS). Albert Einstein arrived at about the same time, and a few years later Kurt Gödel joined, following the takeover of Austria by Nazi Germany. Von Neumann was one of the great polymaths of the age. He made significant contributions to the debate over the foundations of math, which culminated in Gödel demonstrating the inconsistencies underlying arithmetic, as well as to quantum physics, game theory, digital computer architecture, workable nuclear weapons, and, just before his death, self-reproducing automata.

With the coming of World War II, von Neumann was drawn into a number of military research and development projects for the government. One of them was the Manhattan Project, a secret atomic bomb program, based on a remote mesa in New Mexico known as Los Alamos. There von Neumann tackled the problem of predicting a physical process that had frustrated mathematicians since

Blaise Pascal, the 17th-century French mathematician, Christian philosopher, and inventor (who developed and built a number of early mechanical calculators). The problem was how to calculate hydrodynamics, or the turbulent, even chaotic, flow of liquids, such as a mountain stream cascading through rapids. Von Neumann took a very mathematical approach. He characterized the problem first, deduced a novel means of solving it – numerical simulation – then theorized the computer hardware required to accomplish that simulation and the software (which wasn't yet called software) needed to manage the hardware.

Liquids behave like other complex systems, which are resistant to nonlinear equations for characterizing and predicting how they will move through time. In the early years of World War II, von Neumann had become an expert on the mathematics of shaped charges – how to get maximum impact from, say, a bazooka shell aimed at a Panzer tank. At the Manhattan Project he argued for the so-called implosion method of detonating an atomic weapon, in which an explosive shock wave compressed a plutonium core to criticality. The problem was "shaping," or channeling, the rapidly flowing blast of explosives for efficient compression: controlling and focusing it.

Von Neumann's method was to simulate the flow of the blast by breaking it down into tens of thousands of tiny packets and running them through an IBM computer that recently had been delivered to Los Alamos. The scientists programmed into each packet rules that described how it would react to local obstacles and to its neighbors – a kind of algorithm. But the calculation required massive amounts of data to be fed into the computer, which would then calculate each tiny slice of time for each tiny packet. After that the results had to be fed back into the machine to create a simulation of the collective wave. As Richard Rhodes wrote in his history of the hydrogen bomb, *Dark Sun*, the result was "like catching the successive positions of a hall full of dancers with the quick pulses of a strobe." The effort, however, was anything but quick, requiring millions of punch cards and large teams of data feeders working around the clock for weeks on end. The results were still relatively crude, but they allowed von Neumann to design the explosive "lenses" that surrounded the bomb core, solving one of the key problems of building workable atomic weapons.

Computer simulations have a voracious appetite for data and in turn produce massive amounts of new data. Simulations of complex problems require an ever-expanding source of data. And to manage ever-larger datasets, ever-more-sophisticated simulations are required. This set of relationships has driven the development of computers.

The pudgy, talkative von Neumann was at the forefront. At Los Alamos he employed an analog IBM computer that essentially was a large calculating machine. The slow speed of the calculating project inspired him to rethink how computers should be built. Once again there was a practical reason behind his thinking. The so-called Super project to create a hydrogen bomb became a high priority as soon as World War II ended. Led by von Neumann's Hungarian colleague Edward Teller, the Super project used a powerful and sophisticated implosion mechanism in which a fission device acted as the detonating trigger, creating not just a shock wave but a massive wave of electromagnetic radiation that compressed the bomb's deuterium core to such an extent that it initiated a vastly larger fusion reaction.

Among other things, this required a much more complex set of calculations to understand the burst of neutrons and heat set off by the fission explosion. In 1944, on a train platform, von Neumann fell into conversation with an engineer who recently had helped build a computer at the University of Pennsylvania that used vacuum tubes to replace the gears and relays of the IBM machines. The computer, developed by engineers J. Presper Eckert and John W. Mauchly, was called the ENIAC, for "electronic numerical integrator and computer," and it ran the first calculations for the Super bomb in December 1945 and January 1946, calculating the tracks of millions of neutrons through time far faster than the IBM at Los Alamos could.

Soon after, in a 105-page paper, von Neumann described the concept of a stored-program computer. In this device instructions and data could be programmed into an electronic memory, replacing the physical reconfiguration of plugs, relays, and cables – much like an old-fashioned telephone switchboard – required for each change of program. Von Neumann went on to build his own digital computer at the Institute for Advanced Study: the MANIAC (mathematical analyzer, numerical integrator, and computer), which for a period in the 1950s was the fastest computer on earth. The MANIAC was the first stored-program computer – the now-ubiquitous design is still known as the von Neumann architecture.

At the cloistered and theoretically inclined IAS, thermonuclear bomb making was not universally popular. Even the institute's new director, J. Robert Oppenheimer, who had presided scientifically over the Manhattan Project, had qualms about an even larger bomb, though he supported the MANIAC project. However, the computer project was very different from the high abstraction the institute was famous for: applied rather than pure math, engineering over thinking. After the machine became obsolete, in the late 1950s, the institute faculty voted never to engage in such a project again.

Still, von Neumann's profound contribution to computing remains with us today. He managed to build the first universal computer, the kind of machine British mathematician Alan Turing, now famous for decoding the German Enigma code during World War II (and for the movie *The Imitation Game*), theorized was possible in 1936. At the time, Turing was a mathematics student at Cambridge University. In 1935 he had attended a class on the foundations of mathematics that elucidated the same set of problems Gödel had wrestled with. Then he went for a run. While resting in a meadow, Turing imagined a theoretical machine that could prove any mathematical assertion presented to it. Such a machine would process – read and write – a tape containing symbols, which would act as a set of instructions for the device: that is, algorithms processed by an all-purpose computer. The machine was universal because it could simulate other machines when it had what Turing called their standard descriptions. In short, Turing's universal machine was programmable, so he brought the concept (if not the name) of software to mechanical computing devices. Turing received his

Ph.D. at Princeton in 1936 after writing his famous paper "On Computable Numbers." Von Neumann knew both Turing and the paper, and he succeeded in making the Englishman's idea of a universal machine tangible.

At 18 I needed to get a job to pay for my studies at the University of Houston. I'd been accepted at other schools, but Houston was inexpensive and my girlfriend was going there. I answered an ad for a job as an accounting programmer at a company that owned gasoline terminals. I knew nothing about accounting (or gasoline terminals), but I bid on the job and was surprised when I got a call a month later.

There were only two people in the company's Houston office: the president, Rick Worley, and his secretary. The rest of the company was in Mississippi. Rick wasn't bothered by my age. He had put himself through college working on the railroad from midnight to 8:00 a.m., and he had never seen anyone who could program like I could. I started working for him part-time. We would climb into his big Mercedes and drive six hours to Biloxi, Mississippi, where we would spend days installing software and training operators to use it, all the while watching huge gas terminals fill.

I was happy with the job, the programming, the Mercedes, the French fries and burgers on the road, and the discussions about life with Rick, who was a real Texan. He offered me a full-time job, but I turned him down. After my freshman year I transferred from Houston to the University of Texas at Austin, which had – and has – an excellent computer science program. Over the next few years, I studied computer science. We covered Hilbert, Gödel, Turing, the von Neumann architecture, and a lot more. I programmed and tutored math and English. I was always working.

Then, in my senior year, I heard from Bell Labs.

CHAPTER 4

Signal and Noise

"Persistence compounds your ability."

B ell Labs had come to the UT Austin campus to conduct interviews in my senior year, and they made me an offer: They would pay for my master's degree if I went to work for them. At the same time, I had applied to UT's business school, which offered a full fellowship, and I had offers from Bellcore (the research arm of the regional Bell operating companies, which had been spun out of Bell Labs in 1984) and an oil company. But Bell Labs was, well, Bell Labs – a vaunted name in electronics and the birthplace of the fundamental technological breakthroughs that had shaped digital electronics and communications.

Bell Labs scientists have won eight Nobel Prizes since 1937, for everything from the invention of the transistor and the laser to Claude Shannon's theory of communications, with its mathematics of information and noise. In the late 1970s, Bell Labs developed the programming language C, which was the backbone of most of the programming I did, and of the Unix operating system, which runs Apple's Macs, and many other systems, large and small. (And it developed the more advanced version we use today, C++.) After some deliberation I accepted Bell's offer, agreeing to attend UT's master's program in computer science for the 1988–1989 academic year.

It was brutal. For nine months I did little more than study; I got very little sleep. We spent 40 hours a week on computer graphics alone. But academically it was very exciting, allowing me to pursue a focus on computational complexity that I'd begun as an undergraduate. Computational complexity, which studies fundamental problems of computation, was abstract and mathematical and didn't call for a lot of programming, but it did involve a deep dive into algorithms, the mathematical expression of the mechanical steps a computer must take to solve a problem.

I found that to get my mind around a difficult problem I needed a good 48 hours of concentrated thinking – working it and working it. Persistence was critical. And difficult problems were the focus of my master's work. With two other students I wrote a thesis that was a proof of one aspect of what computer scientists call an empty complete set, also known as an NP-complete (for nondeterministic polynomial time) problem. This involved the fact that the time required to solve some problems with a known algorithm grows very quickly – exponentially – as the scale of the problem grows. It would be good to know that an algorithm is NP-complete before you run it and find yourself using lots of processing power. One example of this is the traveling salesman problem, in which you try to solve for the shortest route of a salesman traveling from city to city and then returning to his origin. As you add cities, the problem grows exponentially. This isn't just theoretical. Traveling salesman problems are applicable to complex calculations such as microchip design and coordinating multiple satellites in orbit. NP-complete problems are, in computer science jargon, "hard," though they can be solved more quickly with shortcuts, approximations, and other techniques.

By June 1988, I had finished my studies – the first UT student to complete the computer sciences master's program in a year. Actually, I did it in nine months, but I didn't tell Bell Labs I was done, so I had three much-needed months of vacation before I reported to the company's research facility in Middletown, New Jersey.

But Bell Labs proved a disappointment. The Bell System had been broken up in January 1984, with AT&T and Western Electric, the long-distance telephone business and its manufacturing arm, separated from the local Bell operating companies. With its monopoly gone, Bell tied its research more closely to the business models of its operating units. And by the time I got to Middletown, times were changing for technology companies. The action in digital electronics had swung decisively to Silicon Valley, which was flush with venture capital, start-ups, and dynamism. The internet was coming, and computing was rapidly democratizing as Moore's law took hold, with computing power steadily advancing and moving from mainframes to minicomputers to desktop machines.

The freedom to explore at Bell Labs had been lost – a freedom we try hard to encourage at WorldQuant. At Bell Labs, I felt mired in bureaucracy and process. We generated about four lines of code a day. Everything had to be approved and back-tested. To be forced to slow down infuriated me. It reminded me of the Soviet Union.

I quickly realized that I didn't really want to be a technician and I didn't belong there. It was sad. Luckily, I had made a number of friends there, many of whom felt the same way.

Unsure what to do, I wavered between applying to law school and going to business school. I knew very little about finance or investments. But I had read Connie Bruck's *Predators' Ball*, a book about high-yield bond innovator Michael Milken, and found the subject fascinating. So I applied to and was accepted at Milken's alma mater: the University of Pennsylvania's Wharton School.

Wharton was a revelation. The school was very competitive, and I was exposed to the kinds of people I had never known before. At the start of the MBA program, we all went on a team-building retreat. *The Economist* wrote a story about it, featuring a photograph of a woman who let herself be carried by a group of students to build trust – that was my wrist in the picture. What I found fascinating about Wharton was that when students were asked, they all thought they were above average. About half said they had once saved a life.

In my first year at Wharton, I participated in the AT&T Collegiate Investment Challenge, a three-month stock-picking contest. I teamed up with a former Bell Labs colleague, Richard Hu, who was headed to Columbia Business School. Neither of us knew much about stock picking. But I had an idea, and we managed to climb into the top 12 of 12,000 teams in the challenge, more because we'd figured out how to win the contest than because of our investment skills. Our strategy was to pick the most volatile and correlated stocks and hope that large moves went our way. We were betting solely on luck, but during the competition we did see some four-times gains. This was a lousy strategy for serious investing but ideal for a one-off challenge with zero real-world downside. After hanging near the top of the ranking, we faded. But the contest had a real upside for me: Richard, who grew up in Taipei City in Taiwan and came to America at the age of 16, went on to build WorldQuant's overseas operations.

Wharton exposed me to finance. For a time while I was at the school, I worked at D.H. Blair & Co., a New York firm that in those years was known for dealing with small technology start-ups. My job was to identify high-tech investment opportunities, contact inventors and developers, and put deals together. This was lots of fun, though difficult and time-consuming, and I didn't manage to close any deals. D.H. Blair didn't have the best reputation, but the job taught me the challenges of being an entrepreneur who must confront many unforeseen obstacles between an idea and its successful execution in the marketplace. These entrepreneurs doggedly pursued their goals.

My next job came courtesy of the Wharton placement office. It was brief. I was sent to Moscow by the Harvard Institute for International Development to help Russia's unfolding privatization process, which was being run on the Russian side by economist and politician Anatoly Chubais. The Harvard operation, headed up by the university's Russian-born economist Andrei Shleifer, was advising Chubais. Perestroika had been unleashed, the Soviet empire had fragmented, and the Berlin Wall had fallen. Russia was in chaos. I was intrigued to return to the country my family had fled for the sake of freedom. I thought I might find a home there, given that Russia was undergoing such a dramatic transformation. But after two weeks I knew it wasn't for me. I realized I did not want to spend my working life there, so I returned to the United States. Today WorldQuant has two offices in Russia. The truth is, despite its many political and economic challenges, Russia remains full of brilliant people.

Post-Moscow, I needed a job. I had gotten married. So I resorted to the strategy I often pursued when faced with the unknown: randomness. Through trial and error – meaning, by mailing out thousands of letters addressed to random CEOs – I eventually got a call from Timber Hill in Greenwich, Connecticut. At the time, Timber Hill was a proprietary trading firm founded and run by Thomas Peterffy. (In that year, 1993, Peterffy also started Interactive Brokers, which went on to become one of the world's most successful online trading and trading software companies.) Peterffy was, and is, quite a character. He was born in Budapest in 1944, during World War II, and he was 11 when the Hungarian Revolution broke out against the Soviets in 1956. After studying engineering in Hungary, he fled to West Germany, then, in 1965, to the United States. Like me, Peterffy arrived in New York unable to speak English. He graduated from Clark University, in Massachusetts, then took a job as an architectural draftsman in New York. The firm acquired a computer, and Peterffy offered to program it – even though he knew nothing about programming. But he fell in love with programming, and in 1967 he moved to a firm that was developing early computerized financial models. In 1977, Peterffy invested his savings in a seat on the American Stock Exchange and began years of struggle to get his increasingly sophisticated computerized trading systems accepted by commodity, stock, and options exchanges.

My interview with the company – that is, with Peterffy – was memorable. It took place at his apartment in Greenwich, where his butler (his butler!) served us drinks. I made an offhand joke about programming, and he chided me for not having respect for the practice. He told me: "To be successful in this business, you have to think about it all the time. Lots of people in this business are very smart, but not everyone can think about it all the time." Those words – *you have to think about it all the time* – made a deep impression on me. Peterffy's phrase has pretty much become my motto – at least, it's one of them. At the time, I was struck by how simple and obvious it was. In fact, it was exactly what I did when I was faced with a complex programming challenge.

Despite my poorly received joke, Peterffy hired me. I was assigned to research various computerized investment strategies and write algorithms for them. I had all the tools for this kind of work – the programming skills, the familiarity with algorithms, and an accumulating knowledge of finance and the markets – and at Timber Hill I began to use them with the goal of making money in the markets. However, in Peterffy's eyes I was just a researcher, not a trader. After two years I moved on and joined Israel Englander's New York City hedge fund firm, Millennium Management.

Today I own one of Peterffy's former residences in Greenwich. But I don't have a butler.

∽

For any trader and investor, the great challenge in using computer simulations to model and predict financial markets and securities is the efficient market hypothesis. Formulated by Eugene Fama at the University of Chicago in the 1960s, the EMH, as it's known, dominates finance to this day. Even so, it's been challenged practically and theoretically over the past few decades, including through the kind of quantitative trading we practice at WorldQuant today. (Fama shared the Nobel Prize in economics for the EMH in 2013, not long after the financial crisis, which raised some issues about market efficiency.)

Fama's hypothesis argues that it's impossible to predict future stock prices because current prices contain all the available information about a stock, including assessments of its future price. In short, belief in any method of predicting markets is akin to believing in Santa Claus. The hypothesis suggests that there can be no effective simulation of prices for a given strategy. Because future prices don't exist, simulation must involve past and current data. Thus, the hypothesis breaks any connection between past and future. Instead, markets take the random walk popularized by Princeton's Burton Malkiel in his book *A Random Walk Down Wall Street*. That helps explain why so few active investors or traders beat the market over a longer period of time.

The efficient market hypothesis is a powerful idea. Driving it is the notion that it's very difficult to beat a market full of rational investors, who will efficiently arbitrage away so-called inefficiencies such as mispricings. One consequence is the rise of passive strategies – index funds and exchange-traded funds – which generally make no attempt to beat the market but rather try to mirror it, or sectors of it. Prediction, however, is a stubborn phenomenon: In picking a sectoral index, investors are trying to anticipate which sectors will rise and which will fall. As a result, investors ride the market tide, making the assumption – another prediction – that over a longer period stocks are a good bet. It helps that index funds are extremely cheap, unlike actively managed mutual funds or individual shares bought through a broker. In fact, attempts to pick stocks involve risk for everyone except the broker, who will make money on every trade regardless of whether it proves (purely by chance) to be a winner or a loser. This is not that much different from the strategy Richard and I developed for the AT&T Collegiate Investment Challenge. In the end, we were hoping to get lucky. And we had one large advantage that investors in real markets lack: We had nothing to lose.

The random nature of stock prices, and the first glimmers of the efficient market hypothesis, originally were modeled by a French mathematician, Louis Bachelier, in 1900 in his doctoral dissertation at the Sorbonne. The 70-page "Theory of Speculation" revealed commonalities between markets and natural systems. This seminal paper did Bachelier no particular good as a career move. Linking markets and nature mathematically was viewed as odd, and he struggled to find academic positions. In fact, although Bachelier was a profound observer of how markets operate, he was never an investor or a speculator; he was a pure mathematician. But he recognized that stock prices mimic so-called Brownian motion – the meandering, unpredictable paths tiny particles in still water follow as they are bumped about by the random movement of water molecules in response to thermodynamic background noise.

Bachelier demonstrated that the proper way to deal with such unpredictability was not through a linear equation but through the mathematics of probability. Prediction was difficult, but Brownian motion did conform to certain statistical tendencies – probabilities that the particles, or prices, would end up at a given distance over a given period of time. The way to think about Brownian motion or what we call a random walk was not to view it as an absolute prediction, like Newtonian billiard balls, but to play the odds. Bachelier also quantified the insight that these movements would grow larger over a longer period.

The French mathematician was far ahead of his time. His paper became immensely influential, foundational in a variety of ways, but that happened only many decades later. He derived the formula that led to Albert Einstein's early work on Brownian motion in 1905. Bachelier was also an early explorer of what's known today as stochastic analysis, or the statistical analysis of random movements. Today stochastic processes are used to analyze a broad array of complex systems, from finance and economics to biology, chemistry, and quantum physics to information theory, telecommunications, and computer science. Claude Shannon's 1948 paper "A Mathematical Theory of Communication" wrestles with a stochastic communication process defined by entropy, or uncertainty.

And Bachelier really made the first attempt to calculate the value of futures and options, which makes him a forebear of the Black–Scholes option pricing model. Developed by Fischer Black, Myron Scholes, and Robert Merton in the 1970s, this may be the most ubiquitous model in finance. Many macroeconomic forecasts today employ so-called dynamic stochastic general equilibrium models, or DSGEs, which attempt to calculate the effects of random shocks like changes in oil prices, tax policy, and economic policymaking over time on general economic equilibrium. Like von Neumann's calculations of neutron flow in hydrogen bombs, these complex, dynamic models are normally run on computers. Von Neumann himself developed an early general equilibrium model in 1945, soon after his work on game theory with economist Oskar Morgenstern. DSGE models have since grown much more sophisticated, but they've not proved as predictive as von Neumann's bomb calculations.

Bachelier's insights into markets ushered in a rigorous theory of risk and reward. Financial economists discovered that, over time, certain sectors of the market, such as small-capitalization stocks, tend to generate greater returns than others. But the higher reward from these sectors exacts a toll. They are riskier, in part because they are more volatile. There's always a trade-off between risk and reward.

Enter Fischer Black. He was trained in physics at Harvard and received a Ph.D. in applied math, specializing in operations research, logic, computer design, and artificial intelligence. As Peter Bernstein writes in *Capital Ideas: The Improbable Origins of Modern Wall Street*, his book on the development of modern investing, Black's "main interests were in applying these subjects to methods for processing information." But Black was soon drawn to finance; after a stint as a consultant, he taught at the University of Chicago, then at MIT. He finished his career at Goldman Sachs, making him arguably the first quantitative "rocket scientist" – a trader trained in physics and math – on Wall Street. He provided a sharp contrast to the brash world of the trading floor. Black was quiet, precise, and self-deprecating. (He also could be comically straightforward. At Goldman Sachs he wrote a memo for traders he titled "The Holes in Black–Scholes," then revised it to "How to Use the Holes in Black–Scholes," aptly capturing the difference between theory and trading practice.) Like many advanced financial thinkers, Black took the efficient market as an article of faith, particularly after his tenure in Chicago.

As a result, in 1970 Black was deeply skeptical of one of the most successful proponents of active, or value, investing, Arnold Bernhard of Value Line. The underlying issue: Can investment analysis predict the path of stocks in efficient markets? Value Line adhered to the value investing approach made famous by Columbia University's Benjamin Graham and his student Warren Buffett. The idea is to discover, through a close analysis of company data, stocks that are undervalued – the price of a share is less than it should be based on its intrinsic value – or overvalued. A belief in equilibrium underlies this investing approach, a conviction that because investors are rational, prices will drift toward true value.

Bernhard's Value Line system used market data to target undervalued stocks. Bernhard developed the system himself after he was fired from credit rating agency Moody's during the Great Depression. The Value Line Ranking was literally a straight line that Bernhard superimposed on the target stock price – the true value. The ranking was based on growth of earnings, price momentum, and the price-earnings ratios of each stock relative to the market and historical standards for the stock. In the early days Bernhard actually traced the stock price on a transparency and hand-fitted the value line over it. When the price of the stock fell a certain amount below the value line, he called it undervalued and a candidate to buy. When it rose enough above the line, he urged its sale. Based on this technique, Bernhard discovered that many stocks in 1929 had been significantly overvalued. He broke the system down into five bins, or "ranks," depending on how far the stocks had deviated positively or negatively from their value lines.

At first, Bernhard self-published his rankings in book form. But after trying to interest Wall Street firms in his ideas, he discovered that he could sell regularly updated versions directly to investors. For years Bernhard and his assistants could be found in their offices at 347 Madison Avenue laying out value lines by hand and visually fitting them to individual stock charts with long rulers. In 1946, Bernhard hired Samuel Eisenstadt, the son of Russian immigrants and a U.S. Army veteran who had a degree in statistics from New York's City University, as a proofreader. Eisenstadt went on to make important improvements, including the use of ordinary least-squares regression analysis, and boosted the accuracy of the value line with the cross-sectional analysis of many stocks instead of a time series.

These calculations were far too complex for existing mechanical calculators. So, in the early 1950s, Eisenstadt, who had become Value Line's director of research, bought one of 46 UNIVAC I computers, the first commercial mainframes (a new term at the time). The UNIVAC, or universal automatic computer, was the direct descendant of the ENIAC developed by Eckert and Mauchly at the University of Pennsylvania. Their company had been acquired by typewriter maker Remington Rand in 1950, then led by General Leslie Groves, Robert Oppenheimer's old military boss at Los Alamos. The first customer for the UNIVAC was the U.S. Census Bureau, which helped pay for its development. The computer weighed 13 tons, and its central processing unit occupied 1,250 square feet of space. It performed about 2,000 operations a second, and its memory consisted of 12,000 characters. Data was entered on punch cards, with one instruction per card.

Though Value Line lacked the manpower of the Manhattan Project, the mainframe, combined with Eisenstadt's more sophisticated quantitative methods, produced faster, more detailed, and more accurate valuations, particularly with respect to statistical validation. Nonetheless, academics and the Wall Street research community took an extremely dim view of Bernhard's methods, for different reasons. Academia considered Value Line's performance claims a violation of efficient markets; Wall Street viewed Value

Line as a crude attempt to quantify matters of intuition and professional expertise.

Fischer Black also was skeptical. He believed in strong, efficient markets. "My position has been even more extreme than the strong form of the random walk hypothesis," he wrote in 1973. "I have said that attempts to pick stocks that do better than other stocks are not successful." Black would never fully recant, but he would alter his view in an important way.

In 1970, Black had debated with Bernhard at a Chicago conference, in a session called "Portfolio Management: Active or Passive?" He took the passive side. Bernhard defended the active position by presenting results of a study that showed Value Line's five ranks, from best to worst, performed as expected. Black admitted he was impressed and launched a deeper study using regression analysis, separating returns on the portfolios from the returns of the overall market – gleaning what we now call the alpha from the beta.

Black then wrote a letter to the editor of the *Financial Analysts Journal*, outlining his results. "The net results of the portfolio simulation, assuming transaction costs of 2% or less in and out, was that the [Value Line] strategy continued to give significant results over a five-year period, although the level of significance was reduced somewhat. ... It is always possible, of course, that the success of the past will not continue into the future. It is interesting, however, that since this analysis was originally done, the performance of the Value Line rankings has continued to be as good as it was in the five-year period covered by this report." Black titled the letter "Yes, Virginia, There Is Hope: Tests of the Value Line Ranking System."

The letter kicked up a debate over efficient markets and Value Line that lasted for decades. The Value Line anomaly, as it came to be called (suggesting just how orthodox the efficient market hypothesis had become), has an important implication, which Black understood completely: If the EMH is not fully operational, if all information is not embedded in current prices, then stock prices will not follow a completely random walk. Efficiency may not be strong. Although stock prices may follow a random walk to a large degree, they don't necessarily do so entirely. The randomness of stock prices is like noise that may contain a nonrandom pattern – a signal. By necessity, the violation of the EMH by some fundamental, active, or value investing approaches implies, in theory, that information about future price changes is embedded in the pattern of preceding ones, much as technical traders, with their charts and jargon, argue.

Extracting this signal from the noise isn't easy. Value Line went from Bernhard's hand calculations to Eisenstadt's UNIVAC to (with the rest of the world) successively smaller, more powerful machines. Computers became widespread, then omnipresent. Today anyone can access data from the internet using firms with access to multiple databases and powerful software tools, such as Thomas Peterffy's Interactive Brokers, for a nominal monthly sum. Value Line lost its intellectual edge, though it still exists as a website with a comforting, if optimistic, slogan: "The Most Trusted Name in Investment Research." Bernhard died in 1987.

Value Line appeared one more time in Black's biography. After advising Goldman traders on how to exploit the standard Black–Scholes option pricing model, Black turned to a mispricing that he had been pointing out to his classes at MIT for years. In 1982 the Kansas City Board of Trade launched the first index futures product, which was based on the Value Line universe of stocks. The Value Line index was a geometric average, not an arithmetic one. It was not just the simple average of annual returns, as most traders assumed. It required a calculation of the ratio of one year's stock price to that of the year before. Black knew better. The mispricing was small, but he realized it was significant and eventually would be arbitraged away. In 1984, not long after he came to Goldman, Black showed the firm's traders how to exploit that error. They did, to great profit – reportedly $150 million – before the gap closed (killing the arbitrage trade) in the summer of 1986. Not long afterward, Goldman made Black a partner.

Fischer Black died in 1995 at only 57. Because of his death, he did not receive the Nobel Prize for the Black–Scholes model, won by Scholes and Merton two years later. In December 1985, however, Black, then president of the American Finance Association, gave the keynote address at the group's annual meeting in New York. He called his speech, and the paper that followed, simply "Noise." It was classic Black: to the point, precise, and profound. Much of the paper was a reflection on the nature of markets and trading, and on market efficiency.

At the start, Black contrasted noise with information, and throughout he offered observations on the symbiosis and competition of two kinds of investors: noise traders and information traders. He wrote: "In my model of the way we observe the world, noise is what makes our observations imperfect. It keeps us from knowing the expected return on a stock or portfolio ... It keeps us from knowing what, if anything, we can do to make things better." Because noise is always present, markets are less than perfectly efficient. We often miss inefficiencies because much of trading is trading on noise as if it were information. "The noise that noise traders put in top stock prices will be cumulative, in the same sense that a drunk tends to wander farther and farther from his starting point."

All estimates of value are noisy, Black wrote, so we never know how far price is from value. A market is efficient, he noted, when the "price is within a factor of 2 of value, i.e., the price is more than half and less than twice value." He admitted this was an arbitrary number, but one he felt was reasonable. Based on this definition, he said, "almost all markets are efficient almost all of the time. 'Almost all' means at least 90%."

That's a long way from the strong form of efficiency. Black's observations explain why active or value investing can at times thrive and why there is a place for the kind of quantitative investing I was wrestling with at Timber Hill and Millennium. The noise in the markets may be deafening, but there are patterns – signals, however weak – that information traders can detect and act upon. In short, there are ways to beat the market. But those trades rarely last for very long.

∽

I was on my way. But let me add one story that was quietly unfolding during those years when I was in and out of schools and jobs.

When I was in my mid teens, my father decided to rein-
vent himself once again. After leaving New York for Richmond,
he decided he would become a violin maker. He was an accomplished violinist and knew a lot about what made a superior, even
a great, instrument: the sound box – the wood carefully chosen,
dried, varnished, amplifying the vibration of a bow across strings
into resonant audio waves. But he knew little about making (or
repairing and restoring) violins. Traditionally, going back as far as
the 16th century, when the Amati and Guarneri families and, most
famously, Antonio Stradivari, built magnificent violins in Cremona,
Italy, the process of becoming a luthier involved a lengthy appren-
ticeship with a master. It remains that way today. To be an appren-
tice, you're usually young and unattached, with modest needs that
can accommodate your modest income. It takes years.

My father had a family and another job, and he was middle-aged.
Nonetheless, he was undeterred. Though a beginner, he sat in on
master luthier classes at Oberlin College, in Ohio. At one gig he
found himself next to a cellist who was also a violin maker and
reluctantly agreed to let him assist and observe. "Assist" usually
meant sweeping the floor. In his spare time, between practicing
daily and working, my father taught himself to make violins.

A number of years later, I was having dinner with my business
partner, Izzy Englander, at a restaurant on Manhattan's Upper East
Side. Sette Mezzo is a tiny and unprepossessing Italian restaurant
with an unusually high-powered celebrity clientele, many of whom
live in the neighborhood. A very well-known man came over to our
table, and Izzy introduced me to him.

"Oh, I know a famous violin maker with that name," he said.

"That's my father," I replied with some pride.

Persistence.

CHAPTER 5

Waves

"Take action. Nothing else counts."

The waves of sound my father produced on his viola washed over me as a child nearly every day. In fact, all of us, child and adult, are immersed in waves in their various physical manifestations: sound waves, water waves, electromagnetic waves. There are regularities to waves and a mathematics of waves. Yet we often take waves for granted.

In the 19th century wave phenomena were one of the more fertile areas of discovery across a broad range of fields, particularly classical physics. In the 20th century Viennese physicist Erwin Schrödinger worked out equations for the behavior of electrons that described them as waves, with oscillating, sinusoidal, rising, and falling patterns. At the same time, Werner Heisenberg at Germany's University of Göttingen (home to von Neumann, Hilbert, and other key figures) developed a similarly precise set of equations that described the behavior of tiny atomic particles as points in a field – or matrices, an algebra Hilbert had pioneered. Schrödinger's and Heisenberg's equations were soon recognized as fundamentally related, an effort von Neumann contributed to; they described the same natural, in this case quantum, phenomenon.

Heisenberg then realized that although you could precisely describe a particle's momentum or position, you couldn't do both at the same time. Momentum could be captured in the wave function and location as a point in a field. This was the root of Heisenberg's uncertainty principle: The very act of observing the location of quantum phenomena will affect momentum, and vice versa. We now think of fundamental particles, including photons of light and the electrons of electricity, as sharing the properties of waves and particles, but this counterintuitive concept bothered Einstein until his death in 1955.

Markets also can be seen as waves. Chart a stock or a market and you'll track the rise and fall of prices. Smooth out the charts and they resemble the regular oscillation of a musical instrument or the steady beat of waves on a beach. Sometimes the waves produce a clear tone, or signal, but sometimes they just produce discordant, random noise.

∽

The North Sea is one of the world's densest shipping regions, supporting trade among major developed nations: Norway, Denmark, Germany, the Netherlands, Belgium, France, and the United Kingdom, as well as the other Scandinavian countries, the three Baltic states, and Russia. But the shipping lanes in the North Sea are treacherous. The harsh weather increases the risk of collisions with other ships, with oil platforms – it's a major drilling area – and with land and undersea rock formations. The complex wind patterns, and numerous areas where the sea bottom rises near sea level, generate a surprising number of fierce waves far from land. The North Sea rests upon the European continental shelf. Its relative shallowness provides an advantage in drilling for oil, but it makes the North Sea much more dangerous than the open ocean.

For many years maritime lore insisted that the North Sea had more than its share of so-called rogue waves. According to those who claimed to have witnessed them, these immensely destructive waves were impossible to forecast and seemed to appear out of nowhere. The waves had common characteristics: They often struck in otherwise relatively calm seas (though in heavy seas they could be extraordinarily destructive); they seemed to travel at any angle to the direction of the prevailing winds and the background waves; and they moved fast. They were distinctive in appearance. As the waves approached, water rose up like a wall, with a deep trough in front that since ancient times has been called "a hole in the sea," and another trough behind – fore and aft. Ships in the rogue waves' paths often disappeared; others foundered.

Scientists generally dismissed these stories as fantasies, hallucinations, or exaggerations. Then, on New Year's Day 1995 at 3:20 p.m., a drilling platform in the North Sea, the *Draupner*, was engulfed by an enormous wave. (The *Draupner* was named for a golden ring belonging to Odin, a god in Germanic mythology, that had the ability to multiply itself.) Fortunately, the crew had taken refuge within the rig to escape the severe weather, and although there was damage to the rig's supporting structure, the platform itself stayed intact. In fact, the rig's crew never saw the wave itself.

As part of its routine telemetry, the platform's downward-pointing laser instrumentation tracked the sea swells before, during, and after the wave passed. The maximum wave height was estimated at 84 feet from trough to peak; the single peak was about three times higher than the preceding and following waves. No storm had ever occurred at the *Draupner* with waves anywhere near that size.

The *Draupner* wave provoked a number of studies. "Rogue wave" is now a technical term. Scientists estimate that these waves sink one major ship each year. In early September 1995 (the same year the *Draupner* was hit), a rogue wave in the North Atlantic struck the *Queen Elizabeth II* as the ship was sailing from Cherbourg to New York. Canadian weather buoys measured the wave at 98 feet. The captain wrote in his log, "It looked as if the ship was heading straight for the white cliffs of Dover." The wave broke over the bow, causing an enormous shudder to run through the ship; two smaller shudders followed, attributed to the ship falling into the "hole" on the other side of the wave. The *QE II* survived with minor damage and no injuries.

What causes rogue waves? The most common hypothesis involves multiple smaller disturbances coinciding in one place at one time. You see that at the beach when incoming and outgoing waves combine to create a larger peak, which then bursts. But those waves are formed by the effect of shallow water. They fail to explain the sustained shape of a traveling rogue wave or the deep troughs on either side of it. Though they persist long enough to cause damage, most rogue waves suddenly appear, then disappear. Their shape is distinct, with a flatter face than normal waves. Normal waves propagate in groups and slowly disperse. Rogue waves are solo acts that travel as if they have an appointment somewhere. Other explanations for the phenomenon have focused on tides, volcanism, and wind effects, but all of these hypotheses have shortcomings. Tidal surges are long and flat, there is no evidence of volcanism in large lakes where rogue waves have appeared, and rogue waves have emerged on days without a breath of wind.

One essentially solitary wave is the tsunami. It has an explicitly exogenous cause, created by action from without, such as earthquakes, rather than endogenous action, from within. A seabed suddenly rises as a tectonic plate shifts, displacing a column of water from seabed to surface and producing a potentially deadly ripple of energy. The wave moves with great velocity over a very wide area – the more water displaced, the greater the propagation – and packs an enormous amount of energy. In the open ocean tsunamis are relatively low, solitary elevations. Ships bob over them, barely taking notice. But they wreak tremendous damage when they slam into land. As a tsunami approaches shallower waters, the vertical displacement of water is manifested in two other kinds of motion: The wave rises above sea level and begins to ebb and flow horizontally; impeded by friction, the water piles up even higher. These forces form a giant, destructive breaking wave – a "tidal wave."

But although a tsunami produces a monster wave before it slams into land, it does not resemble a rogue wave in open water. Tsunamis do, however, illustrate some fundamentals of hydrodynamics. Water in waves does not travel forward – the energy of the wave does. The water in waves actually moves up and down. A wave is a vertical disturbance of water that propagates from one position to the next, like the wave of spectators at a football game. Because the medium is fluid, the up-and-down displacement in any fixed location does not generally stop after a single cycle. Instead, because of internal friction, it persists, lessening over time. Think of throwing a small stone into a pond; long after the pebble has dropped to the bottom, smaller and smaller waves ripple out from the point where the stone hit the water.

For many years waves in water were seen as a linear phenomenon consisting of the combination of sinusoidal elements. "Sinusoidal" is derived from the word "sine," which is a serpentine curve, often repeated, like those pond ripples. In this context linear means that if you have two waves, each with different attributes (wavelength, frequency, velocity, amplitude at the peak), and you combine them, you simply add the separate heights of the predecessor waves to calculate the height of the resulting wave. This is simple, intuitive, and wrong, though it explains how scientists have calculated that a wind-generated mid-ocean wave the height of a rogue would occur only once in 10,000 years. But, of course, this doesn't explain the solitary nature of the rogue or its unusual shape. What does cause the traveling rogue wave? Again, recall the tsunami, in which the wave with the greatest displacement of water travels the fastest. Traveling waves are not necessarily linear like two waves colliding in the shallows at a beach; they can be non-linear, with their effects not a matter of addition but of multiplication. Traveling waves, under the right conditions, may produce a wave height that's *greater* than the sum of its parts. Of course, we can't just conjure that extra water out of thin air; it has to come from somewhere. An ocean or a lake has a finite amount of water and energy. If the rogue wave has more water and energy, other waves must have less. What seems to occur in the birth of a rogue wave is that the sinusoidal pattern of the background waves is somehow disturbed, by a gust of wind or a change in the current, and waves begin to pile up. The peak then sucks energy from nearby background waves, creating the trough, or hole. The wave diagram would show shallow, fluctuating background waves; a deep decline followed by a very high peak; another decline; and a return to normalcy.

We now know that this physical description has an underlying mathematical basis. A rogue wave, with a peak towering above its background waves and deep dips before and after, is one solution of the so-called one-dimensional nonlinear Schrödinger equation. This is the same Schrödinger who developed the quantum mechanical wave equation, and, in fact, the nonlinear equation is a variation on that historic piece of math. The nonlinear Schrödinger equation describes a solitary, traveling, sharp-peaked wave, three to five times higher than the background waves. Today it has a name: "soliton," a solitary, self-reinforcing wave that travels at a constant speed over great distances. This particular wave appears only when a number of specific parameters occur. In the ocean the necessary values occur relatively rarely but with some regularity. They produce what are known today as Peregrine breathers. "Breather" is a physics term for a nonlinear wave that concentrates in a localized, oscillatory fashion, "breathing" in and out. "Peregrine" refers not

to the falcon but to British applied mathematician D. Howell Peregrine, the scientist who derived a traveling soliton from Schrödinger's equation.

To be clear, the modulation is tiny, nearly unnoticeable, but the
effect may be enormous – *exponential* – a feature typical of nonlinear systems in general. Scientists have now successfully created
rogue waves in tanks, in a kind of simulation. The wave created in a
tank, or on the open ocean, is not caused by a sudden large motion
but by a small deviation of just the right amount, as described in
Schrödinger's equation. Rogue waves are not the product of the
linear addition of two smaller waves, but of a nonlinear exponential
increase in height triggered by a shift in inputs. Peregrine's nonlinear wave phenomenon also has a close mathematical relationship with work that began at Bell Labs with the invention of the
laser and resulted in the development of fiber-optic communications. Light, too, is a wave that can form sudden traveling peaks –
pulses, or solitons – racing through optic fibers. These can be used
for rapid, efficient long-distance communication. And they can
convey information. D. Howell Peregrine meets Claude Shannon.

∽

What does a bunch of waves have to do with markets? We have
all seen that markets can sometimes behave in nonlinear ways, with
small changes tripping large effects. The efficient market hypothesis
isn't just a case of an overactive academic imagination. Price movements display a large, often predominant, random quality. Markets
consist of a multitude of agents, like photons in a beam of light,
electrons around an atom and molecules in Brownian motion. Markets have a chaotic, or "noisy," quality that produces unanticipated
phase changes. They suddenly veer from a benignly oscillating
pattern – prices gently rising and falling, trending up or down – to
something more violent, more volatile.

The natural reaction to these transitions is to seek an external,
or exogenous, cause – a conspiracy, a policy mistake, a business
failure. But often there isn't one. The cause may be internal, endogenous, just as it is in rogue waves, though it's triggered by exogenous events such as a dip in the wind or an uptick in subprime

mortgage defaults. In financial terms these transitions feature draw-downs or extended rallies. If they're large enough, they're known as bubbles, busts, meltdowns, or crashes. Like a rogue wave or the quant quake, these drawdowns are unanticipated. They travel fast. And they can be very destructive. By the time you recognize them, it's probably too late.

One of the scientists who has cracked open these complex systems is Didier Sornette, a professor at Zurich's Swiss Federal Institute of Technology (where Einstein was both a student and a professor and von Neumann studied chemistry). Early in his career Sornette focused on phase transitions – that is, the sudden shift from liquid to solid or from solid to liquid. From there he began to study how complex natural systems break down. These problems took Sornette from physics to geophysics to finance and econom-ics. He saw the same pattern from the physical world replicated in human processes such as markets and economies.

In the early 1990s he tackled the problem of predicting when Kevlar pressure tanks on the European Space Agency's *Ariane 4* rocket could suddenly (and calamitously) rupture under stress. He patented a prediction algorithm, then applied his method to earthquake prediction. A few years later Sornette and his col-leagues noticed that financial crises could be viewed as "ruptures" in the market. In all three cases – rocket pressure tanks, earth-quakes, markets – Sornette detected an accelerating pattern of oscillating waves leading up to what's known as a critical event: a log-periodicity pattern in which the time between discrete events decreases with the logarithm of time – that is, in factors of 10 rather than the linear one to two to three. Log-periodic oscillations were signals, edging the door open to the possibility of prediction.

"It is striking how both randomness and patterns seem to coex-ist in these [market] time series," Sornette wrote in a 2003 book on market crashes, *Why Stock Markets Crash*. He argued convincingly that markets are complex, nonlinear systems that demonstrate "coherent large-scale collective behaviors with a very rich struc-ture, resulting from the repeated nonlinear interactions among its constituents: the whole turns out to be much more than the sum

of its parts." Major drawdowns occur rarely but far more often than
the efficient market hypothesis would suggest.

That is, there is some order in chaos.

∞

Before I went to Wharton, I had little idea of what went on in
markets, investing, or finance – not to say how to predict regular-
ities in complex, self-organizing nonlinear systems. I learned a lot at
Wharton, but I didn't really get a crash course in the markets until
I began doing investment research at Tom Peterffy's Timber Hill.
Before that I was just a programmer with a business degree.

Peterffy had hired me as a researcher, and that's what I did:
programming, model building, and investment research. At Timber
Hill there was one person who mattered, and that was Peterffy. He
was a brilliant guy, but he owned the company, and everything
emanated from him. After about a year I felt the need to move on. I
had some ideas and I wanted to trade. I didn't really know where I
wanted to go, so I resorted to my random strategy. I began sending
out letters again to CEOs – thousands of them. (By then I'd learned
that you can't just dump a giant batch of letters in one place; you've
got to split them up and put them in different mailboxes or the
mailman gets mad at you.) One day I got a reply from a headhunter
representing a hedge fund firm called Millennium Management.

For four months I went back and forth interviewing with
Millennium. Basically, what I had was an idea based on some
notion of exploiting end-of-day trading patterns, where aberrations
occurred in prices as traders closed out their positions just before
the market's close. This was my first alpha. I described it to the folks
at Millennium – including the boss, Izzy Englander, though up until
then I knew nothing about him – and laid out the idea. The algorithm itself, the formula, would remain proprietary to me, but that
was fine with Izzy. Millennium made me an offer.

Still, I couldn't decide. I was trying to be scientific about it, using
the analysis methodology I'd learned at Wharton. Later, Peterffy
said to me, "You're trying to choose between two unknowns, one
greater than the other." But if I did nothing, I realized, nothing
would change. Eventually, I turned to my old friend, randomness.

I flipped a coin. I was going to stay at Timber Hill. I told Izzy, and he promptly talked me out of it. Timber Hill then tried to get me to remain, employing an argument similar to the efficient market hypothesis: "You already know a lot about us, so you must be more valuable to us than to anyone else."

Peterffy called me into his office. The O.J. Simpson decision was just being announced on television. He asked me what I thought. "Innocent," I said, because the jury's deliberation had been quite short. He said, "How sure are you?" I said 60%. He said that if I wanted to be a trader I had to be 100% sure, but being right 60% of the time was okay. He predicted that Simpson would be declared guilty. When we heard the verdict, Peterffy shrugged and said he couldn't do anything to match my offer. So I told him I was leaving.

It was the best decision I ever made, albeit with a little assistance. I learned a lesson about decision making and cutting losses. *If you have to decide and you can't, flip a coin. If it's the wrong action, you'll feel it and reverse course. Actions have a compounding effect; it's bad to deliberate for too long.*

Going from Timber Hill to Millennium was a major career move. You can't imagine two more different places, although both would become remarkably successful. Timber Hill was a single, suit-wearing entity, a reflection of Peterffy; Millennium was a collection of mostly independent traders. Izzy Englander was encouraging and helpful; he wanted you to succeed for him, for the firm, but you had to do it yourself. He was, and is, a good judge of people. He could see right into you, like an X-ray.

At the time, Millennium wasn't that big. Izzy had founded it only six years earlier, and it ran out of two rooms in a building at 111 Broadway, next to the Trinity Church cemetery off Wall Street, with about 30 or 40 people. The whole fund had about $100 million. The firm ran a bunch of different strategies, from merger and statistical arbitrage to pairs trading. You worked pretty much on your own. On one side of me was a guy who put up a giant sheet of cardboard so I couldn't see his computer monitors; on the other side was someone we called Hot Sauce Dave because he liked to put hot sauce on everything he ate.

But when I got to Millennium, I had a problem. On my first day at work, my alpha lost $5,000. I felt terrible and apologized to Izzy. He forgave me, but he offered a succinct version of his own philosophy: "Keep losses small. Profits will take care of themselves." I was able to make changes in the alpha, deriving a working strategy out of the original idea. It was a good lesson in the benefits of actually trading, not just testing. In fact, parts of the alpha worked and parts of it didn't, so I took out the parts that didn't work, and the rest was fine. You can simulate all you want, but the reality is what happens when you trade, and that knowledge provides an important edge. Later I would discover that everything typically works at a 50% or lower level as it moves from simulation to actual trading.

I quickly learned the culture Izzy had built. At Millennium you either made money or you left. When you made money, you felt good, and when you didn't, you felt bad. I worked totally alone in my first years there, focused on my alpha: one man in a small boat on a vast and endlessly changing market. I focused intensely on making that alpha work. Peterffy's belief in always thinking about problems made a real impact on me. I owe him for that rule. It's so simple, like all good things. The mind is a muscle, and it has to be exercised. I found that I enjoyed this because I knew it was my edge. I also began to view the stock market differently. No matter what the economy does, there will *always* be a stock market. Stocks will *always* move. So there are *always* ways to make money in the market. The market will yield to thinking plus effort plus ability. It's a clean arena, albeit a risky one. There's no need for personal connections.

Within a few months the alpha was making money. Another trader, who had been helping me, tried to absorb me into his group. I protested and Izzy prevented this from happening. I decided to expand my strategy. My second alpha was a pairs-trading strategy. In the office I'd heard talk about pairs trading – matching up a long position and a short position in two highly correlated securities, a technique first developed in the 1980s at Morgan Stanley by Nunzio Tartaglia and Gerry Bamberger – but I didn't really know enough to make that work, as I was about to discover.

When Russia suddenly devalued the ruble and defaulted on its debt in August 1998, my positions tumbled. The first alpha held up, but the second did not, and I lost most of the year's gains. I had to dig myself out, day by day by day. Izzy was encouraging, but others told me I should just quit. Trying to make money with alphas was too hard, they said.

But I dug in. In those days I had time to mull over where I had been and where I might go. No one, except perhaps my family, would care if I failed. I was on my own. I lived many hours every day in the mental world of algorithms – that is, step-by-step rules. If this, then that; if not X, then Y. That may be the genesis of the rules I began to formulate for my own life.

Blame no one else. Minimize regrets. I had to accept responsibility for what happened to me, even if it wasn't all my fault. This realization was empowering, causing me to focus on action, on things I could control. Whatever happened, happened; I needed to retrieve the information and move on.

Don't compromise. Play to your strengths. Did I have weaknesses? Certainly. But it seemed a waste to spend time on those weaknesses rather than on improving my strengths. Weakness can only be improved marginally, but strengths can be improved proportionately more, given how much time you spend on the effort. Don't spend time bemoaning what you lack.

Obstacles are information. If you can't get something to work, there's a reason. What's the reason? Maybe it's a bad idea. Learn, adjust, reattack.

So I chose, like my father when he struggled to become a maker of violins, to persist at trading. And soon I began to climb out of the hole.

CHAPTER 6

Correlation

"Without specific, quantifiable goals, movement through life is Brownian motion – random."

Fortunately, my first alpha made money for a decade – a long time to beat a strongly efficient market. I learned to create algorithms that selected trades that worked, and this provided me with a lot of proprietary information that no one else had. The alpha itself was volatile and not a smooth signal, and it required a strong stomach. At times the portfolio was very volatile. I continued to work alone. Isolation may have been necessary, at least for me, but it's difficult over a long period of time. Traders rarely last if they work by themselves for too many years.

I spent many hours thinking about that alpha, turning it over in my head. How could it be improved? How could I maximize returns while minimizing drawdowns? How could I test it more effectively and learn from the market? The 1998 Russian default lurked in the back of my mind as a warning about how the market could suddenly turn against you. At the same time, I deepened my understanding of the market and the capabilities of alphas; I struggled to research more alphas. I was vaguely aware that other people were working in the same vein, but I was focused intensely on my own alpha and its possibilities.

Again and again I was reminded of the merits of persistence; Peterffy was right. I tried to *aim for the anxious edge,* to push myself to the point of mild anxiety. Too much degrades performance; too little means you're not doing enough. Sometimes, as I turned over a problem in my head, I couldn't sleep and I would force myself to run five miles. Your body is responsible for your insomnia. It will observe its punishment and be scared to do that to you again. I realized how easily *arrogance distorts reality.* Arrogance makes you perceive the environment in a way that maximizes your ego. But the environment does not exist for you, so your perceptions turn into fiction. You make bad decisions by chasing illusions. These destroy the favorable conditions that led to the arrogance in the first place. Think Nebuchadnezzar or King Lear. Pride goeth before a fall.

And then there was the virtue of *economy of expression.* I had never been particularly talkative. But I saw that good traders thought efficiently. Efficiency implies clarity and economy of thought, and this shapes the way a person communicates: tersely, precisely. Pretend you have a fixed number of words in your life. The sooner they're all said, the sooner you die.

The financial use of the word "alpha" goes back to 1968, when Michael Jensen, then a young Ph.D. economics candidate at the University of Chicago, coined the phrase "Jensen's alpha" in a paper he published in *The Journal of Finance*. Jensen's alpha measured the risk-adjusted returns of a portfolio and determined whether that portfolio was performing better or worse than the overall market. Eventually, Jensen's alpha became known simply as alpha.

Hedge funds adopted the word to describe what they aimed to deliver to investors: above-market returns. In the quant world alpha morphed into a shorthand for the algorithms or models used to predict the prices (or relative prices) of securities. There are a number of ways to define an alpha, nested within one another like Russian dolls. An alpha is an algorithm, a combination of mathematical expressions, computer source code, and configuration parameters (that is, the software and hardware setup). Like any algorithm, an alpha contains rules (for example, an if-then rule, where a decision is made conditional on an event X occurring) that the computer executes, and which aim to predict the return on financial securities. There are an infinite number of ideas about the market, each of which *could* be an alpha. We develop, test, and trade alphas because even if markets are operating efficiently, something has to drive prices toward equilibrium, and that means opportunity will always exist. In broad terms investors are always trying to achieve returns that rise above the background noise of the broader market, and their activity moves prices, nudging them toward intrinsic value.

That sounds straightforward, and fundamentally it is. But although the idea embedded in an alpha may be straightforward, the computing tools and data we use to implement that alpha are a lot more complex. For instance, an alpha can be represented as a matrix of values, varying through time and indexed by security (we call these time-varying structures vectors). The size of the vector can be large when the goal is to produce forecasts for the thousands of securities we trade in markets around the globe. Each day the software reevaluates the logic underpinning the alpha idea and populates the vector with new values based on market conditions. The alpha's performance can be evaluated by examining the historical daily returns of an idealized portfolio constructed using the alpha forecasts. The ratio of the average daily return to the (estimated) daily volatility is something we call the information ratio of the alpha. That ratio measures the strength and steadiness of the signal and tells us if an idea is working – whether the signal we're seeking is robust or weak. The information ratio indicates whether we are dealing with a signal or with noise.

This may seem arcane. In fact, much of what we do in quantitative investing consists of using probability and statistics to tilt the odds in our favor. Keep this in mind. A major focus when we build, test, and invest in alphas at WorldQuant is to reduce or manage correlation – that is, a mutual relationship or connection between two or more things. We strive to produce steady returns that beat the broader market. We aren't looking for home runs, and we try very hard to avoid disasters.

Going for the big score, as Richard Hu and I had attempted back in 1992 in the AT&T Collegiate Investment Challenge, often involves a bet that you will catch a market wave and ride it. It's based on luck. But the trouble with luck is that it can be good or bad, and at WorldQuant we don't like the odds of the latter. One of our major goals is to avoid the rogue wave that can suddenly swamp us. We want to minimize the effect on us of significant market drawdowns – sustained declines like those investors suffered during the Russian default, the dot-com bust, the quant quake, and the financial crisis. But that doesn't mean we won't act aggressively – the key rule here is to *take minimal risks and manage losses*. Aggressive behavior forces your environment to react to you, rather than the other way around. You're in control; you have a wider array of options and a higher probability of success. But you need an exit plan if it doesn't work out.

∞

Let's return to the North Sea, where the winds are still blowing, the sea is still angry, and risk is an ever-present factor, to tell the story of a ship, an errant wave, and a failed, if illuminating, attempt at risk management. The ship belonged to a privately held Norwegian shipping company that specialized in supply vessels for deepwater oil-and-gas drilling platforms. The company's founder was Peter Lorange, a Norwegian economist who had taught at Wharton and MIT's Sloan School of Management and served as president of both the International Institute for Management Development in Switzerland and Oslo's BI Norwegian Business School, the second largest in Europe. His company was a small player, with only two vessels, but the ships were complex and expensive, and losing one would be catastrophic.

Lorange was an exceptionally sophisticated owner. He had a degree in operations management from Yale University and a Ph.D. in business from Harvard, and he understood risk. One of his company's biggest risks was engine failure in the North Sea that could leave his ships at the mercy of the waves. So Lorange undertook a cost-benefit analysis. His calculations showed that five engines on board each vessel reduced the risk of total – that is, simultaneous – failure to an optimal level, given the associated costs of purchase and maintenance. His assumption was that two engines were generally active at one time, for speed and maneuverability, but if one failed, a single engine could propel the ship successfully in the severest of storms. Lorange's backup redundancy was therefore five times what was necessary: All five engines would have to fail for the ship to be threatened. What were the odds of that? Well, some of those odds turned on "time to failure" statistics for diesel engines at sea. How long would a diesel engine operate before it began to break down, particularly given the rigors of the sea environment? The odds of one engine failing within one year were roughly one in 1,000, or 0.001. The odds of all five failing were .001 to the fifth power, or one chance in a quadrillion. That was pretty comforting.

However, on a calm day in 1992, one of Lorange's ships was sailing the North Sea when a large wave struck it at an odd angle. The damage was minor and no one was hurt. But a small fire ignited in an electrical panel just outside the control room and burned for 20 minutes before the crew found it and put it out. By then both engines had died and the remaining three could not be started. The ship drifted dead in the water. Fortunately, other ships were in the area, and one towed it into harbor for repairs.

Was this the one chance in a quadrillion? The ship was equipped with high-powered, well-maintained diesel-electric drives, much like the engines on diesel locomotives. These engines generate electricity, which is stored in batteries that drive the propeller shaft. The storage batteries were in one location, and the control wires to all five engines ran through a conduit a few inches in diameter. The fire broke through the conduit, disabling the engines. The odds of this happening had nothing to do with the independent risk of all five engines failing. The odds were not independent but coupled, and what looked like five separate events was actually just one event that affected the five engines simultaneously.

This story illustrates a number of tendencies that contribute to what Yale sociologist Charles Perrow has called "normal, or system, accidents." Perrow writes in his book *Normal Accidents* that this term is meant "to signal that, given the system characteristics, multiple and unexpected interactions of failure are inevitable." He pinpoints two systemic tendencies that often lead to catastrophe: a high degree of interactive complexity, with lots of interconnected parts, and tight coupling among those parts. Catastrophes, Perrow writes, have always been with us. What's new is that today "we produce designs so complicated that we cannot anticipate all the possible interactions of the inevitable failures." Operators can't alleviate the problem because the system is incomprehensible to them.

Complex systems that are not highly coupled may break down, but in those cases the problem may be more limited in scope. (The trade-off is often between the efficiency a coupled system may display and the safety of the system: A tightly integrated system may be optimally efficient and very risky, with a breakdown spreading quickly.) Coupling refers to components of larger systems that are dependent upon each other. If one fails, the other shuts down as well, like the ship engines' electrical system disabled by a fire.

Coupling, in this usage, is roughly synonymous with correlation.

∽

Risk management on the North Sea and the humble leek would not seem to have much in common, but thanks to modern finance they do. The leek, a vegetable with a mild, onion-like flavor, resembles a miniature tree, with a root end planted in the soil, a fleshy white bulb, and a stalk with a green, thatch-like top. Not all parts of the leek are equal in the eyes of cooks, be they high-end chefs or simply people who prepare meals at home. The root end is inedible and usually sliced off and tossed in the compost heap. The long stalk at the top is flat and dry and often discarded as well. The best part of the leek begins in the white bulb and runs into the pale green middle.

So leeks are not perfect. Even the best leeks – the ones that a high-end chef might pay a princely sum to buy – have parts that will be discarded, and even the worst have parts that can be used. This leads to a conclusion: The optimal return for a leek farmer would result not from selling the whole leek but from marketing the best parts to fancy chefs and the worst parts to less picky, budget-minded home cooks. How could this be done? By rebundling the leek harvest into large packages, lining up the root ends, then using a cutting machine to slice the vegetables perpendicularly. You'd end up with various slices – or, in French, *tranches* – of all the leeks. You'd discard the roots and stalks as useless, leaving tranches that started with the highest-quality white bulb and dropped in quality as they moved up the increasingly green stalk. This "synthetic" leek bundle of tranches could be sold to customers instead of the entire leek. Customers could buy what they wanted and what they could afford.

What we're really describing here is a practice that has grown increasingly common in finance: securitization. Replace the leeks with thousands of mortgages and you have a mortgage-backed security. The process of turning mortgages into a synthetic security is roughly the same. Pools of mortgages are packaged and sliced into tranches by quality: those with a higher risk of default at one end, those deemed safer at the other. These tranches are then sold to institutions with varying appetites for risk, from banks that often are required to buy only the highest-quality mortgages to more speculative investors that are willing to shoulder higher risk to generate higher rewards. The theory behind this bundling is that each tranche is independent of the other, like the backup engines in Lorange's ships, or the various leek slices, or, significantly, coins that are being flipped.

The architects of mortgage-backed securitization assumed that the likelihood of one mortgage defaulting would be minimally related to the risk that a second mortgage would default. In particular, the mortgages of one tranche, like jumbo loans, would have little to do with the mortgages of another – say, subprime loans with no-doc applications. They believed that mortgages were essentially uncorrelated. Unfortunately, the 2008 financial crisis proved that assumption disastrously wrong. In fact, these mortgages were a key part of a large, highly correlated housing market with valuations at record highs and lots of leverage. The default risks within and among the different tranches turned out to be tightly coupled, as was the larger global financial system.

To put it another way: If the default of one mortgage significantly influences the fate of another, or if there is a common cause for the default of both, the separation into tranches provides only the illusion of safety. The tranches become identical to the original loans and are in sync, rendering the clever reallocation of risk a fantasy and the pricing for all the mortgages wrong.

That's the danger of correlation. It's as if a black fungus infected a whole package of leeks – good, bad, and average – spreading from one vegetable to the next.

As in the case of Lorange's ship, procedures designed to mitigate and distribute risk may sometimes increase it. In the years leading up to the financial crisis, some relatively sophisticated investors believed that securitization reduced or even eliminated risk, thus allowing them to pile on more risk. This disregard for risk because you believe you are protected from its consequences is called moral hazard. Meanwhile, the faith that the risks seemed to be isolated from one another masked the reality that the engines of the global economy were actually wired to one another. The financial crisis demonstrated that correlation existed on every scale, from individual stocks to financial derivatives to entire economies. Investors learned that components of systems we never suspected to be related were in fact coupled and correlated.

The world missed this because the system was so large and the coupling so complex that no one really saw the destructive correlations. And many people fooled themselves, believing that so many others couldn't be wrong.

To do well in quantitative investing, you must use simulation with great care to minimize correlation. There are psychological traps common to investing, such as believing that a pattern in the data is a rule decoding some aspect of market behavior, when actually it may be mere chance. You must be brutally honest, minimizing ego and wish fulfillment. This gets harder as you grow more successful and hubris slips in. It isn't good enough to simply produce a lot of ideas or to believe that they will work, like my Wharton classmates who all thought they were above average. These beliefs have to be ruthlessly tested for evidence of correlation.

Nearly everyone in investing practices some form of backtesting, running an investment or model through a variety of databases of historical data. True, some investors have more and better data than others, and this makes a difference. But while backtesting is vital to alpha production, it can produce a seductive sense of security – and result in a moral hazard. It's a cliché, but past results don't always guarantee future results. The simulation process must begin with a variation of the UnRule applied to alphas: Many alphas are duds, and no alpha will last forever. In probability terms every alpha falls somewhere between "0," meaning it never works, and "1," meaning it always works.

Like quantum physics and gambling, quantitative investing is all about the mastery of probability and statistics, a subject that's widely taught these days but difficult for many people to grasp. Quantitative investing is a numbers game. Once again, some of the techniques key to quantitative investing are rooted in the nuclear weapons programs during and after World War II, in particular the work of John von Neumann and one of his closest colleagues, collaborators, and friends, Polish-born physicist Stanislaw Ulam.

After the war Ulam left Los Alamos and the Manhattan Project to teach at the University of Southern California. There he succumbed to viral encephalitis, a brain infection that almost killed him. He recovered, but barely. His doctors told him to rest and avoid mental activity, so he took up Solitaire. Soon he was trying to calculate the odds of a game of Canfield Solitaire, a variation of the popular card game with a low probability of playing out. After trying to figure the odds-on combinations of the 52 cards – the calculations exceeded even his world-class math mind – Ulam adopted a different approach, playing out 100 games and counting the number of successful plays. This was a rough-and-ready simulation, an approximation, but Ulam realized that it grew more accurate as he played more games. He quickly recognized the applicability of the technique to some of the problems plaguing the ongoing hydrogen bomb project. "It occurred to me then that this [method] could be equally true of all processes involving the branching of events," he wrote in his memoirs.

The branching Ulam had in mind involved neutrons released by the atomic explosion initiating the hydrogen bomb. These neutrons had a number of finite options. They could scatter, be absorbed, change their velocity, or produce more neutrons by splitting a nucleus. This sort of branching, which frequently seems random, occurs often in nature, usually before some abrupt phase transition. Didier Sornette's Kevlar tanks exploded when tiny fractures suddenly proliferated in a kind of branching pattern that he also identified in the signals produced by tectonic plates under stress or by markets before a crash.

Thus was born the Monte Carlo method, a name one of Ulam's Los Alamos colleagues, Nicholas Metropolis, came up with as a secret code name. (Monte Carlo was a cheeky reference to the casino in Monaco where Ulam's uncle used to borrow money from relatives to gamble, but it also was a more serious acknowledgment that nature operates, at least in part, through probability.) Ulam and von Neumann worked out the math, and von Neumann saw that the probabilistic trajectories of a random sampling of individual neutrons – several thousand would suffice, in his estimation – could be calculated on the most advanced computer of the day: the ENIAC, by then relocated from the University of Pennsylvania to the Aberdeen Proving Ground in Maryland. (Although there's some controversy over who first thought of the idea, von Neumann did suggest to the ENIAC engineers a way of retrofitting the computer to include stored programs that could more efficiently run the Monte Carlo simulation; this anticipated the Princeton MANIAC's stored-program architecture.)

In his book on the development of computers, *Turing's Cathedral*, George Dyson captures the power of the Monte Carlo method: "Monte Carlo opened a new domain in mathematical physics: distinct from classical physics, which considers the precise behavior of a small number of idealized objects, or statistical mechanics, which considers the collective behavior, on average, of a very large number of objects, Monte Carlo considers the individual, probabilistic behavior of an arbitrarily large number of individual objects, and is thus closer than either of the other two methods to the way the physical universe actually works."

Monte Carlo methods have a variety of applications in finance, from valuing portfolios, options, and derivatives to judging the risk in long-term, complex projects. Beginning in the late 1940s, a flurry of improvements were made to the original von Neumann algorithm by the likes of Enrico Fermi and Metropolis, among others. Monte Carlo opened the door to phenomena that could not be easily calculated using more conventional methods, even on rapidly advancing computers. Monte Carlo and related methods are stochastic processes, using randomness and repetition to capture complex, fluidly changing situations. The output is a set of probabilities, not certainties. This group of stochastic processes shares Ulam's initial observation: The more games played, the closer the approximation approaches reality.

The use of random elements to bring order to a seemingly chaotic system also plays a key role in a statistical theory known as the central limit theorem (CLT). Monte Carlo can be used to simulate reality; the CLT is a key technique to analyze it probabilistically. The CLT was first postulated in the early 18th century by French mathematician Abraham de Moivre, then rediscovered and popularized by another, more famous French mathematician, Pierre-Simon Laplace, in 1812. Francis Galton, an English Victorian polymath and a pioneer of eugenics, called it "the supreme law of Unreason" in 1889, recognizing the paradox of order from chaos, reason from unreason. He wrote, "Whenever a large sample of chaotic elements are taken in hand and marshaled in the order of their magnitude, an unsuspected and most beautiful form of regularity proves to have been latent all along."

The central limit theorem posits that randomly generated multiple samples from a much larger universe will produce a normal distribution of probabilities – a bell curve. Although it has developed a vast number of applications, the CLT is most famously central to polling, which takes a relatively small number of samples and assumes the sum will converge on a normalized distribution that closely approximates the larger population. You can test the validity of the theorem with an easily accessible tool from your pocket: If you flip a coin 10 times, the outcome may favor either heads or tails, skewing from the theoretical probability of 50–50. But if you flip the coin 100 times, the result will move toward that 50% – the central limit. If you do it 1,000 times, the outcome will probably be even closer.

A similar approach can be applied to trading. If you trade a small number of stocks, you run the risk of severe losses if even one of them takes a serious tumble. A number of hedge funds with concentrated positions discovered this in the past few years. (Of course, given the positive relationship between risk and reward, a concentrated portfolio may at times produce high returns.) If you trade a portfolio of stocks, many of which are correlated, they will tend to move up and down together; as a trader you can do either very well or very badly. But if you trade a large number of stocks that are uncorrelated, you can harness the law of large numbers to your benefit. First posited in the 16th century, the law of large numbers is a principle of probability that plays a role in Monte Carlo simulations and states that the more experiments you run, the more the solution will converge on the expected value. In a casino the more a gambler bets on the roulette wheel, the more the overall results will tend to reflect the outcome anticipated by the casino – invariably in the house's favor. In investing, results will converge on intrinsic value.

Consider two simplified trading situations. In one you invest $10,000 in a small number of securities for 250 days, taking gains and losses as they occur. You do pretty well. You win on 55% of your trades and you rack up gains of 60% for the year. The commonly used Sharpe ratio, which measures risk-adjusted return, is 1.63 – excellent for a general investor. Just for comparison, the Sharpe ratio of a Treasury bill, which is as close to risk-free as you can get, is zero.

In real life, however, this portfolio might be a little difficult to live with. It's quite volatile. Though it does finish the year well, if we take a slice of that period – say, day 27 to day 103 – we get a very different view: In that period the portfolio fell by 20%. Moreover, consider another way of looking at the strategy, using a Monte Carlo simulation. Take the 250 price changes and randomly shuffle them 10,000 times, creating 10,000 different hypothetical trajectories for the basket of stocks. Then analyze the drawdowns in those trajectories. We discover that there are 3 chances in 10 that during the 250 days you'll experience a 10% or greater loss in the initial value of your investment, and 1 chance in 20 that you'll lose 20% or more. That's more like gambling than investing.

Now consider a slightly different investment program: 10 different, randomly selected strategies invested at the same time and run for 250 days. Although the overall return is slightly lower than the single strategy on day 250 (an arbitrary end point), at 34% it's still impressive. The Sharpe ratio is now much higher, 3.11, indicating that the volatility or risk is much lower. As a result, the probability of loss is much smaller. There's a 2 in 10 chance of a decline of 2% during the year and a 4 in 10 chance of a 1% drawdown. Here the law of large numbers drives toward two different expectation values. The first value is the expected compounded return over the trading period. The second is the expected variation in the daily returns, which will approach zero.

Because the 10 strategies were randomly selected, they have an unrealistically low correlation. Because of that, the smoothing effect on returns is exaggerated. Still, the example does illustrate just how a properly noncorrelated portfolio of strategies will reduce risk while generating more stable returns.

For me in 2000, with only two alphas, and despite the large number of securities that could be built into them – thousands, of all kinds, traded in exchanges around the world – it wasn't always easy to exploit the full smoothing effect of the law of large numbers. But I had begun to ponder a process that could begin to produce a lot more. I had begun to dream about scaling up.

CHAPTER 7

Scaling Up

"Knowledge grows from knowledge, and good ideas constitute new knowledge, altering reality in the process of growth."

S **cale**. The *Oxford English Dictionary* lavishes more than a page of dense verbiage, broken down into 10 definitions, on this word. Among other things, a scale is a device for weighing; a thin, hard outgrowth of skin in fish and reptiles; the act of skimming a stone across the water; the use of a ladder to surmount castle walls; or, more generally, to climb a mountain, a flight of stairs, or, like the biblical Jacob, a dream ladder connecting heaven and earth.

That ladder and those stairs are significant. The "scaling ladder" metaphorically translates into a means of measurement and calculation. The *OED* also defines scale as "a series of graduated marks on a straight line or curve, representing a series of numerical values, used to measure distance, temperature, quantity, etc.; *spec.* the equally divided line on a map, chart or plan, which indicates its scale and is used for finding the distance between two points." That definition covers everything from the rising and falling notes on the musical scale to mathematics: "any of the various conceivable systems of notation based on the principle that the value of a figure varies in geometrical progression according to its serial place, but distinguished by the number chosen as a radix, base or unit of multiplication."

The concept of scale was familiar to the ancient mathematicians, who carefully studied the stars, then speculated about the smallest of material components, atoms. Those thinkers, who pondered mathematical patterns in nature, mentally traversed heaven and earth, the mind-bendingly large and the very small. Anyone who has dealt with exponents or moved decimal points to achieve a greater or lesser scale knows how math can manipulate scale – how easy it is to soar from the infinitesimal to the cosmic, even the infinite. The universe as we know it, from quantum particles to galaxies, is a graphical illustration of scale and its mysteries.

My initial impulse to scale up my one-man quant desk at Millennium was a lot more prosaic. My first alpha was performing well by then, and a second or third would, in theory, double or triple the money I could make and reduce the risk. So I began working on more alphas, hoping to invest more assets under management and bring in more profits. Of course, there was risk in these ambitions – there always is. My first attempt to diversify with a pairs-trading strategy had failed in the Russian default, forcing me to rework it. In fact, I refocused the pairs-trading approach from a broad strategy to a more highly defined alpha. I also expanded the first alpha quite a bit. But that raised other challenges.

An alpha contains many moving parts. Though it is automated – we could never trade so many securities without automation – the process of monitoring an alpha, as well as back-testing it, not to mention developing and programming it, takes a lot of time and effort. Some think that a quantitative investment is just "programmed" trading, an automatic response to some market change, or nothing more than trading at lightning speeds. Those are fallacies. Man *and* machine must work together. Automation vastly expands what traders can do, allowing a leap in scale, scope, complexity, and productivity that investing had never previously imagined possible. But people – creative, brilliant people – are still essential.

Over this period my trading operation was not specialized at all. I was the researcher, the portfolio manager, and the programmer for both the simulation machinery and the trading infrastructure, and a trader with many active positions. Later all those functions would be defined and we would hire specialists to handle them, allowing us to develop vastly more alphas and to bundle them into strategies more creatively and effectively. What ties together the researcher and the portfolio manager functions? Researchers develop predictive ideas that could become alphas; portfolio managers aggregate those alphas into strategies. But both the alphas and the strategies undergo the same rigorous, repeated back-testing, which is the spine of the operation.

But I'm getting ahead of myself. At this point, these distinctions existed only in my head. I was doing everything with my handful of alphas. I was working pretty much all the time. Some days I'd have an assistant run the system so I could focus on programming or research. I worked on a number of alpha ideas, constructed algorithms, then back-tested them. None of them was particularly good, but I kept trying. During this period my children started to arrive; today there are five of them.

I wasn't discouraged when the ideas I tested didn't work out. The two alphas I was trading continued to perform well, and that kept my spirits up. And I learned through failure. The fact is, every failure or obstacle provides you with information. It's a positive – you absorb that information and move on. You're like a person doing push-ups – the more you do, the greater your strength is and the more you *can* do. That's how I viewed this. If confronted with uncertainty, *act*. It's better than choosing to do nothing. If it doesn't work out, close your position and readjust. I also learned that imitating another trader or firm – whether it was someone at Millennium or another quant fund, nearly all of which had a hundred times my own capital – seemed to doom me to failure. I needed to do it myself. In a brutally competitive arena, where alphas could die when trades grew crowded – when many traders often had the same brilliant idea – there was good reason to think for myself. Imitation was always a danger.

I was developing a more sophisticated sense of what worked and what didn't. Now many of these lessons seem very basic, particularly compared with what we can do today. There were two large classes of price signals: momentum and reversion. Momentum refers to the tendency of stocks to continue on their current track, up or down. Reversion signals suggest a price is either too high or too low and is moving toward some equilibrium. In my experience there were many more usable reversion signals than momentum signals. Much of what my first alpha did was exploit reversion signals at the end of the trading day. The cause and effect were obvious: Traders needed to sell to get liquid, and prices would fall.

Momentum has fewer strong signals. If momentum were greater than reversion, that would imply that prices would move slowly and steadily to an intrinsic value, like soldiers marching from point A to point B. Empirically, that isn't what happens. In reality price discovery is an endeavor that proceeds by making errors that translate into under- and overreactions.

I was also learning to use probability in a more sophisticated way. I began building key components into my simulation program. At Millennium and the quant firms, traders pursued a bundle of arbitrage strategies: statistical arbitrage, merger arbitrage, fixed-income and mortgage arbitrage, relative-value trades. "Arbitrage" refers to the simultaneous purchase and sale of assets to take advantage of a difference in price – for instance, between two different bonds or the shares of two merging companies. Or the trade might involve two different kinds of securities – mortgages, say, and stocks – or similar securities trading at different prices in different markets. A profitable arbitrage can crop up because of some inefficiency in generally efficient markets. That inefficiency is a signal.

Pairs trading, around which I built my second alpha, exploits discernible tendencies of stocks, such as mean reversion. Pairs trading involves two stocks; stat arb employs hundreds or thousands. What makes both of these strategies work is the fact that in some way – very simple or very complex – the securities are correlated. For instance, a pairs trade might involve two correlated stocks, one that a trader thinks will rise – one he wants to go long, or buy – and one he believes will fall, which he can short. Perhaps you are convinced that automaker Ford Motor is overvalued after a large recent move in its share price, while rival General Motors is undervalued because of undue concerns over its pension liabilities, which have sent its shares tumbling. You might go long GM on the belief that its stock price will rebound when investors realize their fears were overblown, and short Ford. You can profit regardless of what happens to the auto sector or the market overall as GM and Ford both move closer to their true values.

But there's another benefit to this type of strategy: risk management. Remember the Value Line system developed by Arnold Bernhard? It had five buckets of stocks, ranging from those expected to rise the most to those that probably would rise the least or even fall. Because Value Line assessed the value of the stocks cross-sectionally – that is, with respect to the market as a whole – the worst-performing bucket was expected to fall in price relative to the broader market. An investment strategy might therefore involve buying the stocks in the top category and selling the stocks in the bottom one. Both sets of stocks would tend to be broadly correlated with the movement of the broader market, like ships rising and falling on the tide, driven by complex underlying economic forces. Normally, when investors try to predict the future behavior of a stock, they are also, deliberately or unknowingly, attempting to forecast the trend of the broader market. This often proves to be a problem because most market prognostications involve finger-in-the-wind hunches. But there's a way to eliminate the risk of the market. In the Value Line example, you can neutralize the market by simultaneously buying and selling the same dollar amount of stocks in the two buckets – hence the term "market neutralization." If the market rises, even just enough to cause the bottom stocks to rise, the gains at the top will outpace the gains at the bottom. Your investment wins even though you didn't place a directional bet on the market.

These neutralization strategies operate through probability; you're playing the odds. They won't score all the time, but they allow you to stack the odds in your favor, giving you a quantifiable edge over time.

In my years at Millennium, I began to learn how to apply neutralization to my simulation programs: The same dollar amounts were invested both long and short on anywhere from 100 to 4,000 stocks. When you're dealing with that many securities, you need to automate as much as you can. Increasingly powerful computers allowed me, like John von Neumann, to build simulations that would have been unimaginable in the past. I was able to handle a much larger number of securities, enabling me to exploit the law of large numbers, and an ever-increasing variety of data. But I needed to build a trading infrastructure that could automate many of the complex tasks of trading so many securities in so many venues. In time, I also found ways to neutralize not just the market but the effects of market sectors, industry groups, currencies, and more. In those days I did the programming myself. These neutralization programs demonstrated the power of the simulation.

∞

By 2000, I had put the Russian default behind me and was aggressively researching different strategies. At the time, I still didn't fully realize the sheer diversity of strategies to explore. I did recognize that my continuing dependence on those first two alphas was a major risk; diversification into other alpha strategies could provide both greater profits and smoother returns. But I faced some challenges. On the positive side I was just glimpsing the possibility of exponential growth: Knowledge begets knowledge, and data begets data. On the negative side I understood there were limits to working alone in addition to the psychological stress and the danger that, without even knowing it, I might find myself thinking like everyone else. And the sheer work of mastering and managing a handful of alphas, let alone 10 or 100 – as fantastic as that seemed at the time – also posed an exponential leap.

I needed help.

We never hired just to expand. There was no overarching plan. It was much more organic, and opportunistic, than that. *Life is unpredictable.* That's a rule I learned many years ago, perhaps as long ago as when my parents announced that we were leaving the Soviet Union. Events don't unfold as anticipated, so there is a limit to what can be planned. The key is to take action: Create the dots, connect them later, because you don't know what will materialize. By creating opportunities, then opportunistically taking advantage of outcomes, you maximize success.

We expanded when I found talent. Early on I hired one assistant, then another. Hiring more people could produce its own challenges – I had to manage them and train them. Also, when you have valuable intellectual property, you need to remain careful. One of my assistants left, saying he was going back to college. Instead, he went to another firm with one of our programs. The issue was quickly uncovered and he was fired by his new employer.

But I kept an eye out for talented people, and when they became available, I hired them. They brought their own skills and began building trading systems and developing alphas, informed by their training, individuality, interests, and intelligence. This, too, was an incremental process. I recruited Jeff Miller, who had been in the NYU math program and at Goldman Sachs, and Brian Johnson, a math Ph.D. and lecturer at the University of Chicago. There were others. Finding smart people with the skills we needed wasn't easy; in the following years I would spend a lot of time thinking about that. Exponential growth often is very slow at the beginning, barely discernible, but you have to build the foundations.

When Geoffrey Lauprete, who today is WorldQuant's chief investment officer, joined Millennium in August 2003, after earning a Ph.D. in operations research from MIT and working at Deutsche Bank as a quant, the group had six people, including me. We were still running only a handful of alphas. Three years later, in December 2006, as we prepared to launch WorldQuant, we had 19 alphas. A year later we had roughly 150, then, a year after that (in the midst of the financial crisis), about 1,000; by 2010 we had nearly 5,000. But we were just beginning. We steadily hired more people, but nowhere near the rate of our alpha growth; this translated into very large productivity gains. New brilliant minds brought new ideas about alpha development and portfolio strategies. I continued to run my own trading book through 2008 but eventually had to give it up in order to focus on managing WorldQuant. I had a lot of other tasks to handle. Like Adam Smith's pin factory in *The Wealth of Nations*, we were beginning to specialize. More important, the curve of alphas was beginning to bend upward.

For most of this period, there was no master plan. The advances were incremental. In a way, we were functioning like the market itself – a sort of daily experiment that tests prices and ideas, culling some and rewarding others. I'd developed certain skills, a certain approach, and some powerful technology, particularly simulation software, which we worked steadily to improve. We added more and more datasets, and the more ideas we pursued, the more we learned about what worked and what didn't. The effort was informed by our increasingly sophisticated grasp of probability and risk management. It really was true: Failure was a kind of success.

We had grown quite successful – though we knew success could disappear in a moment. Sometime in 2005 or 2006, I'd begun to talk to Izzy about spinning WorldQuant out of Millennium. In 2005, Millennium had opened an office in Old Greenwich, where I lived. My group occupied cubicles there, with my glass-walled office taking up about a third of the space. As we expanded, we moved the walls steadily outward, and my office shrank in proportion to the whole.

I'd harbored a desire to run something on my own for some time, and I'd thought hard and long about what we might be able to do and how we could grow the business. I had long defined rules for myself. But now I began to formulate rules for a growing business with increasing specialization. *What makes a good trader?* Intelligence, focus, action orientation, and the ability to learn from errors; economy of words and thoughts, honesty, and a strong sense of self; the ability to take risks, compartmentalize, and handle setbacks without the ego getting crushed. *What makes a good researcher?* Creativity, tenacity, attention to detail, intelligence, relentlessness, follow-through, and, in our case, top-level programming skills. *What makes a good manager?* Empathy, intelligence, creativity, relentlessness, and follow-through. Many of these virtues overlap: relentlessness, creativity, intelligence. We sought out quantitatively trained people who displayed these traits.

I came to believe in two further rules that might appear paradoxical but don't have to be:

> *Scalability.* I wanted WorldQuant to be scalable. A good business runs itself. You create this by choosing the right people. A lot of your effort must be invested in that activity. As a result, it's vital to develop optimal compensation schemes. If that's done well, you need only add more pieces to grow.
> *Minimal bureaucracy.* We aimed to be as flat organizationally as safely possible. Time is money; time is scarce. Bureaucracy wastes time and loses money. If you have the right people, the right systems, and the right compensation schemes, you can scale up without a huge addition of bureaucracy. Many processes in both business and research have an exponential payoff over time. Wasted time produces even greater losses in an exponentially growing operation.

In my vision we would retain a strong link to Millennium, but we'd have our own name and our own way of doing things. Later in 2006 we agreed to move forward. WorldQuant was launched in January 2007. Soon I began to look for a larger house in Greenwich for my growing family.

∽

There's another meaning of "scale" or "scaling" that I was starting to explore in those years. "Scaling simply refers, in its most elemental form, to how a system responds when its size changes," writes Geoffrey West, a theoretical physicist at the Santa Fe Institute, in his book aptly titled *Scale*. Searching for alpha signals is a kind of exploration of market dynamics, seeking islands of order in the midst of turbulence. Markets contain many paradoxes: predictability from random, even chaotic, nonlinear systems; order from chaos; signal from noise. Man-made markets are as much a part of nature as beehives or ant colonies. These phenomena contain many agents, whether they're free agents or hard-wired to behave deterministically, whether they're buzzing flowers for pollen or seeking investment returns. The swarm intelligence displayed by beehives arises not from individual agents, which operate at one scale, but in the hive, from increasing scale. The rules of intelligence that drive hive behavior are fully understood by none but distributed among all.

Nature is full of spontaneous, albeit complex, order, including regularities you can observe through probability and scale. Their harmonies arise from neither a known composer nor a conductor; there appears to be no central master controller. Perhaps the most all-encompassing example is Darwinian evolution powered by natural selection. Change occurs at the molecular, cellular, organism, species, genus, family, and ecosystem levels. These levels can be complex, fluid, and prone to continually shifting conditions and feedback, which over millions of years and many generations shape and reshape life through an essentially orderly, if seemingly random and unpredictable, mechanism: chance mutations driving evolution, nature as experimentalist. We now can glimpse major mechanisms of that order, down to the biochemical machinery of DNA.

Markets have existed only since agriculture developed in the Neolithic period, roughly 10,000 BC. Some 6,000 years ago the Sumerians recorded accounting information on clay tablets, suggesting that the kind of exchanges that lie at the heart of markets had emerged. Prices were probably fairly random. Indeed, until recently the markets, like the ecosystem, were too complex and seemingly too chaotic to fully understand and predict – though they were full of people convinced that they could. But over the past 50 years or so, we have begun to untangle the laws that underlie complex systems, whether we're looking at the weather, evolution, or the markets. We can discern a variety of patterns, or regularities, that extend across these complex systems, even though we don't always know *why* they exist.

Consider so-called power laws. A power law expresses a fixed statistical relation between two quantities, such that a relative change in one quantity creates a proportional change in another. As animals scale in size, for instance, their metabolisms grow more efficient at a set rate. In terms of the math, metabolism grows three units for every four units of weight: A whale is more efficient metabolically than a mouse. If that relationship is plotted on an X-axis and a Y-axis, it produces an upwardly rising slope of 3/4s.

Power laws are eerily ubiquitous once you look for them, in nature and throughout the man-made world (in the physical and social sciences, respectively), effectively erasing the line separating nature from man. Often that proportional change is a fixed exponent, or *power*. Gravity weakens by the power of two with distance; the area of a square quadruples as the sides double. Many phenomena – from the size of cities in a country to the distribution of craters by size on the moon, the frequency of words used in a language, the magnitudes of earthquakes, the names in a population, or the booms and busts in a market – appear to be ranked according to power laws. That is, the data approximates a straight line, or slope, on a logarithmically scaled graph rather than randomly scattered points.

Broadly stated, power laws suggest that many phenomena scale themselves into *hierarchies*. There are many more tiny villages in France than small cities; far more small cities than larger, regional ones; and, by size, only one Paris. (Actually, the largest cities break with what's known as scale invariance; they are, like rogue waves, outliers, larger than they should be, a phenomenon

Sornette dubbed "dragon kings" that describes both major cities and global market meltdowns.) We've known that the distribution of incomes in an economy or companies by size seems to be ranked by a power law since the late 19th century, when Italian economist and sociologist Vilfredo Pareto worked out what's known as the 80–20 rule: 80% of wealth is controlled by 20% of the population, an inverse relationship of two. (Pareto also coined the term "alpha" for the slope of that line.) The principle has been found to work in a variety of situations, such as betting and fixing computer bugs. Pareto himself discovered that 80% of peas are found in 20% of the pods. Even various aspects of the internet – the number of visits to a website, the number of pages, the number of links on a page – appear to order themselves by a power law.

Power laws often apply to complex systems or networks that produce a spontaneous order from apparent chaos. Driving that self-organization are random fluctuations that are amplified by positive feedback. At Los Alamos, Ulam and von Neumann theorized that self-reproducing cellular automata – simple cells or robots with on-off states and the ability to propagate depending on certain fixed rules – evolve through random interaction in extremely complex ways. Others, notably John Conway with his Game of Life (a simulation in which each cell contains a universal Turing machine), have since conducted fascinating computer "games" exploring the evolution of cellular automata.

In the 1970s, Benoit Mandelbrot used computer graphics to show that you can create complexity with self-organizing principles from a few simple rules. He called these fractals, visual representations of scaling that he detected in natural phenomena such as coastlines, tree branches, blood vessels, the pattern of fractures in Sornette's Kevlar vessels, cauliflower and broccoli (which can be chopped up and, unlike leeks, still resemble micro versions of the original macro vegetable) – and in the financial markets. These fractals are self-similar: As you move up the scale, the hierarchies mirror each other, like capillaries and large arteries, twigs and mature branches, and market pricing charts. Mandelbrot's fractals capture the scale-invariant, hierarchical, self-similar, and self-organizing nature of nonlinear, complex systems. Power laws are the mathematical expression of that self-similarity and fractality: order beneath complexity, diversity, and seeming randomness.

Though two of his uncles were well-known mathematicians, Mandelbrot was by nature an outsider, rendered rootless by history and predilection, a self-described misfit and maverick. He was born into a Polish Jewish family that in 1936 emigrated to France, where he entered school and struggled to elude the Nazis. After the war he traveled to the United States to pursue a master's degree in aeronautics at the California Institute of Technology. Mandelbrot returned to France and earned a Ph.D. in mathematics from the University of Paris; by 1953 he was back in the U.S., at Princeton's Institute for Advanced Study (IAS), where he was von Neumann's last postdoctoral candidate. (Mandelbrot, who spent the year at IAS sampling word frequency distributions, admired how von Neumann "had accumulated a number of people who were not part of the Princeton pigeon holes," writes George Dyson in *Turing's Cathedral*, while observing that among the visiting scholars, "everybody else had the dreadful feeling that this may be the best year of their life, so why wasn't it more enjoyable?") He returned to Paris, married, then headed back to the U.S., unhappy with the emphasis on pure math that prevailed in the French capital. Instead, he took a job at IBM. Although Mandelbrot did his most important work at the American computer company, he remained active in academia, teaching at Harvard and finishing his career as the oldest tenured professor at Yale. He retained dual French–American citizenship.

Throughout his very long career, Mandelbrot, like Sornette, was drawn to the complex dynamics of the markets.

He often made the point in his papers and books that fractals reveal areas of order within unpredictable, chaotic markets. Markets scale, he observed, and all price charts look alike if you strip away the legends: A century, a decade, and a day are essentially indistinguishable. Given that, we don't have to seek a comprehensive, God-like understanding of how markets function. That's probably not possible anyway – a reality, Mandelbrot notes, that quantum physics discovered about the physical world a century ago.

But at WorldQuant we can use our alphas and our back-testing systems to find and explore those islands of order, however temporary. For Sornette that order provided the means to begin to develop algorithms to predict what long had been unpredictable: catastrophes such as earthquakes, volcanoes, burst pressure vessels, and market crashes.

At WorldQuant our alphas seek out signals – regularities – in markets. For a number of years, we didn't delve deeply into topics like power laws. We were seeking out, step by step, alpha by alpha, more traditional signals. But we began to recognize how power laws apply to nonlinear systems characterized by positive feedback – that is, correlation. If a market or a population of voters is completely random, you can generate a pretty accurate approximation of the distribution of data along a bell curve. But our empirical experience tells us that markets are not totally random. *The (Mis)behavior of Markets: A Fractal View of Financial Turbulence*, Mandelbrot's 2004 book on markets (co-authored with Richard Hudson), argued that markets have strong and weak memories that undercut the random, coin-flipping quality of the random walk. "Examples of such simple patterns, periodic *correlations* [*my italics – I.T.*] between prices past and present, have long been observed in the markets – in, say, the seasonal fluctuations of wheat futures as the harvest matures, or the daily and weekly trends of foreign exchange volume as the trading day moves across the globe."

One stock may be correlated with another stock or with another security, like a bond; what happens on the New York Stock Exchange may ripple through to London or Tokyo; what happened yesterday, or 50 years ago, may influence today and tomorrow. (At the very least, this insight underpins the validity of back-testing.) This positive feedback, whether it produces mean reversion or momentum or patterns caused by seasonality or the flow of news, is exactly the kind of signal we try to stalk and capture in alphas. As Mandelbrot writes, "Price changes are very far from resembling a bell curve." Our task as we build our alphas is to discriminate between true correlations and those that appear because everyone believes they exist.

CHAPTER 8

An Exponential World

"Make everyone benefit."

O ver the years I stayed in touch with Richard Hu, my friend and colleague from Bell Labs. After Columbia Business School, Richard went to work for one software company, then acquired another, which he refinanced, relaunched, and successfully sold. For five years he worked at a New Jersey consulting firm, advising technology companies on strategic management. I had long wanted to work with him again. As I planned the spin-off of WorldQuant from Millennium, I talked to Richard and asked him what he'd like to do if he joined the new firm. He asked me, "Have you ever thought about opening an office in China?" Richard was born in Taiwan and was interested in the significant opportunity to hire great talent in China. I considered his question, and we hired Richard.

The China of 2006 wasn't the China we know today. The country was growing rapidly, but Westerners who visited would come home and talk about how primitive much of it appeared – how far China had to go. Some of our group were skeptical. But while we planned the spin-off of WorldQuant, Richard immediately moved to Beijing and started recruiting researchers. Though quant jobs didn't really exist in China, he found a lot of intensely motivated, extremely bright young people trained in math and science. Because we were early on the scene, we were able to get the first pick. Later Goldman Sachs and other firms would arrive and begin to recruit, but for a while Richard was pretty much alone. It was like having the only alpha in town.

Richard interviewed a thousand or more applicants. We initially offered jobs to five. Perhaps there's a power law in those numbers: Many of that original group remain at WorldQuant today. Richard lived in China for seven years before moving back to Taipei to run our international operations and serve as our chief research officer.

The China initiative may have seemed an off-the-cuff decision on my part. But I wanted Richard at WorldQuant, and if he saw something in China, I was willing to go along. Again, it was an incremental step, based on the needs of the moment. But it changed everything. We were already beginning to develop alphas in the U.S., based out of our New York and Old Greenwich offices.

The China initiative reinforced the name of our firm: WorldQuant. At the start, China was just an experiment, but it led directly to our increasing emphasis on attracting very bright people who had trained under rigorous educational systems but had relatively few opportunities to use their talents. We had stumbled on a kind of arbitrage. Although China, with its massive population, was exploding as a global economic power, its financial markets were just developing and its investing industry was nascent. Brilliant minds and few opportunities – we would take this strategy on the road.

China, then India in 2008, then many other far-flung locales made possible the concept of the alpha factory. The alpha factory resulted from the potential I saw in scaling up our still quite small group. We had been building alphas one at a time, like handmade furniture. We'd learned a lot about what worked and what we were looking for, but although the numbers were increasing and I was pushing our technologists to automate, automate, automate, you had to look very closely to see any significant scaling.

By 2007 we had hired a tech team to begin developing more advanced tools, starting with our simulation software. When I was trading alone, I'd programmed my own simulation program in C, the general-purpose language developed at Bell Labs in the early 1970s; the tech guys dubbed it IgorSim. Now we needed a simulation system that everyone could use. In 2008 we rolled out WQSim, which employed the then-popular C++ language. Later, on top of that, we built an internet-based simulator called WebSim. We've continued to work on our simulation engines for a decade now.

We knew WQSim was working when new hires who were proficient in physics and math but didn't have a clue about finance and the markets began developing alphas within a month or two of arriving. Another sign came when some of our most senior traders put their legacy research and alphas on the shelf and began building portfolios with alphas developed in China.

We had discovered a powerful formula for growth, and Richard had struck a rich vein of talent. We channeled this talent into researching alphas. To feed our simulators, we found ever more datasets, moving beyond financial data to gather input from everything from news feeds to social media to satellite imagery, opening new avenues for researchers to explore. To keep track of an increasingly complex system, we invested in sophisticated automation for archiving and revaluing positions. At the same time, we took the first steps to automating the very creation of alphas. We began using algorithms that could find signals in the data, then feed them through the back-testing simulator. (We can generate a lot of signals this way, but many of them are noise and lack the predictive power of real alphas.) Within a few years we had transformed WorldQuant from a small furniture shop to Henry Ford's car assembly plant, and productivity exploded. That was the alpha factory.

This system ignited exponential growth in alphas. By the end of 2010, we had more than 13,000 – pretty impressive. Our quant rivals generally had fewer alphas (though many of those alphas performed incredibly well for long periods of time). At the end of 2011, we had archived more than 26,000 alphas; in 2012 we had nearly 60,000. We were doubling every year. Then the curve leapt ahead exponentially. By the end of 2013, we counted some 425,000, nearly eight times more than the year before. Twelve months later we were back to a little more than doubling alpha development: We broke a million. Then we seemed to "slow," hitting 1.7 million in December 2015.

But by the end of 2016, we had developed nearly 4 million alphas, blowing through a goal I had declared internally in 2010 to hit 1 million in five years. I think a lot of people at WorldQuant, particularly some of the veterans, thought I was crazy when I set those goals. Indeed, I wasn't sure we could reach them. But I knew it was worthwhile to put a really ambitious, quantifiable goal out there for people to strive to meet, particularly in an environment that appeared to be driven more and more by exponential growth. And, in fact, we did make it. In 10 years we had gone from 19 alphas to 10 million.

My latest goal, set in 2016, is 1 billion alphas.

That wave of alphas drove WorldQuant's evolution. Mounting numbers of alphas fueled increasing specialization – in research, portfolio strategy, technology – which in turn helped us bring our smart, scientifically sophisticated but financially inexperienced new hires up to speed more quickly. We realized that *trading can be broken down into small processes and taught.* This realization – this rule – runs against what many people in the trading business have long believed. We discovered that most things can be taught; therefore, most things can be learned if you have students who are intelligent and motivated.

With more alphas to choose from, we could package them into portfolios. Today a typical portfolio may contain tens of thousands of alphas; the largest may contain 100,000. To our portfolio strategists, individual alphas, which may have vectors of hundreds or thousands of securities, remain black boxes. The algorithms, logic, and intellectual property remain with the researchers; the strategists know individual alphas only as mathematical expressions of a market signal. As a result, portfolios are not shaped by taking a macroeconomic perspective or exploiting some notion of value. Instead, a portfolio is all math: How does the combination of its alphas perform in the market? What are its characteristics? Can it be improved?

Obviously, what makes it possible for this kind of complexity to function at a high level is the automation we've built, which allows strategists to closely monitor portfolios that may be traded in the market for a few months or a few years. But automation isn't everything. Strategists retain a degree of discretion. They can make "transformations" in alphas – applying risk controls, filtering out certain aspects or changing capital allocation, capital weights, or trading venues. And portfolio strategists must make the call to pull a portfolio and replace it with something new. Strategists are ultimately responsible for the firm's profit-and-loss statement.

Our China initiative provided more benefits than just an accumulation of alphas. For one thing, it reduced the risk that we would fall into the trap of groupthink. Just like when I was trading alone, I worried about unconsciously thinking like everyone else. It's a difficult tendency to battle, and you never know if you're slipping into a well-worn rut. The UnRule always looms: *All theories and methods have flaws.* How can you be sure you're not repeating yourself or locked into ways of thinking that arise from your academic training or deeply ingrained cultural blinders? How do you know that the very fact that you've become more financially sophisticated doesn't make you part of a crowd that will arbitrage any returns to zero – or worse?

You want hungry people who have the persistence and relentlessness to work through difficult problems, who are intellectually independent and creative. But you also need the kind of creativity that you may be able to acquire only if you seek out people with very different experiences, from very different cultures. In advanced math and science, a lot of the best work comes from folks in their 20s, who tackle problems with fresh eyes and perspectives and who have energy and drive. To get them you often have to travel to where they live, whether it's Budapest or Tel Aviv or Mumbai or Moscow. Today WorldQuant has more than 25 offices in 15 countries.

Of course, none of this was a given at the start. The WorldQuant spin-off was a gamble. China was a gamble – the firm was just getting started, and the country would be, at best, a cost center. Would our effort there pan out, and how quickly? I knew we had to treat a project like China as a trade and be prepared to cut our losses if it failed to generate a return over a reasonable length of time. But very quickly it became apparent that China was going to generate a competitive advantage for WorldQuant.

In retrospect, this globalization of WorldQuant makes perfect sense, given my own story, my struggles and triumphs, and those of many of my colleagues. No one could foresee all this, of course, including me when I had that conversation with Richard about moving to China. The decisions were always incremental, going from A to B to C, often based on incomplete data. But setting goals was important. Understanding that we needed to think differently, exponentially, was essential. I knew we wanted to scale up in a very big way and that we had some of the technical tools in place to do it. So we did.

∽

WorldQuant grew steadily. We still can't predict where this growth will take us, but we continue to seek new ways to attract and hone talent in places where opportunities for young math and science folks are scarce. Not long after the financial crisis receded, we pulled together strategies aimed at broadening the recruitment and training that we had begun in China. We made investments to scale the operation, embodied in the exponential growth in our alphas. We wanted to move beyond just finding new talent and opening offices, though that would continue.

I began to think hard about improving education, particularly in quantitative fields. In a sense WorldQuant was always in the education business, training science and math whizzes in finance. I decided upon a multifaceted effort separate from the company itself in which we would offer scholarships to boost the critical thinking skills required for quantitative finance; award grants to support outstanding organizations in math and science around the world; collaborate with nongovernment organizations, universities, and governments; and host meetings and support conferences to encourage greater access to education. And I identified innovations, new research fields, and potential breakthroughs I could support and encourage through venture investing.

In 2009, I set up the nonprofit WorldQuant Foundation to carry out a number of those strategies. At the start the foundation contributed to organizations, such as universities, that teach math, physics, and quantitative analysis. Eventually, we expanded that program to include individual scholarships, mostly in the quantitative sciences. Although there was no direct benefit to WorldQuant from these scholarships and grants, I believed that anything we could do to encourage the growth and development of quantitative science would benefit the industry.

And we weren't alone. In 2012, German computer scientist Sebastian Thrun and two partners started a company called Udacity that was pioneering so-called massive open online courses, or MOOCs. Thrun had led a group that built robots in the mid-1990s, starting with Rhino, a robotic museum tour guide, which served as his dissertation at the University of Bonn. At the Stanford Artificial Intelligence Laboratory, he oversaw the team that developed Stanley, a self-driving Volkswagen, which won the U.S. Defense

Advanced Research Projects Agency's Grand Challenge in 2005. Two years later Thrun joined Google, where he co-founded the search engine giant's secretive Google X research-and-development facility, which produced the driverless-car program now known as Waymo. *Fast Company* magazine called Thrun "arguably the most famous scientist in the world – and perhaps only Elon Musk bests him in successfully persuading regular people to embrace wild ideas."

One of Thrun's wild ideas was to break down the barriers to an elite education. Even before leaving Stanford he had explored the possibilities of online classes that could reach beyond the physical university. He taught his first online class, on artificial intelligence, in 2011 from his living room, using a digital camera and handheld napkins instead of a chalkboard. Some 160,000 people signed up. As *Fast Company* reported in a 2013 profile of Thrun, when the computer scientist ranked the scores from the first exam, none of the top 400 came from Stanford. After moving to Google, Thrun set up Udacity to produce MOOCs, particularly on topics at the inter-section of statistics and computer science.

At the WorldQuant Foundation, we were thinking along the same lines. I also hoped to reach a large, global audience, and to identify and encourage talent, which could be done via the inter-net. And I wanted to teach the kinds of math and science that I believed were reshaping the world. There was a significant overlap with Udacity in content – AI, machine learning, statistics, computer and data science – although we were more focused on quantitative finance and the Big Data necessary for producing alphas. Thrun himself was candid about the challenge of getting students to finish and pass courses, a common problem with many online educa-tional efforts. By 2013 we had begun work on our own MOOC for alpha development. We hoped to offer the course either for free or for a nominal fee to whomever wanted to participate, anywhere in the world. A number of WorldQuant employees volunteered to help generate content.

That initial course was like my first alpha or our China effort – the start of a larger, more complex, unfolding strategy. We took the possibilities of online education in two directions. First, in 2014 we launched the WorldQuant Challenge. Like the AT&T Collegiate Investment Challenge, the WorldQuant Challenge is an investment contest, but one with a strong educational component. It's focused on developing high-performing alphas. Contestants sign up on the WorldQuant Challenge website. We make our WebSim platform available to anyone who enters; they get to use some of the same datasets and back-testing as our researchers and portfolio strategists – pretty radical for the often secretive quant business. (We've even made WebSim available on a smartphone or tablet.)

We use the Challenge as an educational platform and to identify talent, running courses and sessions on aspects of alpha development both online and in meetings around the world. In July 2017 we held 32 such events, ranging from online classes on "financial and technical indicators" and "alpha quality and over-fitting risk" in India to Alphathon information sessions in Korea, Russia, and Vietnam. ("Over-fitting" refers to algorithms that may be excessively complex and thus poorly predictive. An Alphathon is a seasonal alpha challenge.) Participants with winning alphas receive a prize – as much as $10,000 – and we offer the best-performing contestants consulting positions in our research programs; we now have more than 700 research consultants. One participant from rural Taiwan had earned an engineering degree but, because of political considerations and his desire to retain ownership of his family's land, had instead become a farmer. He excelled at the Challenge, and we offered him a role as a research consultant.

Second, we began to plan WorldQuant University. We already had been giving scholarships to traditional universities through the foundation, but I wanted to scale that up. Eventually, we built an entire curriculum in quant finance, with live instructors, around a two-year online master's degree in financial engineering. The university officially launched in 2015 as a nonprofit funded by the WorldQuant Foundation. Again, there is no direct benefit to WorldQuant. I had two goals: First, to eliminate location as a barrier; most of the graduate-level courses in financial engineering are in the U.S., limiting their accessibility, but WorldQuant University can reach any region with access to the internet. Second: to eliminate the barrier of cost; these conventional academic courses can charge $100,000 or more. Educational opportunities often remain a privilege rather than a right, and I wanted to do something about that. I strongly believe that lack of money should not determine students' educational options or limit their ability to access high-quality resources or work with experts in the field.

We accepted the first WorldQuant University class in 2016: 200-plus students from more than 35 countries, including Nigeria, Kenya, China, and Russia – proof that while talent is evenly divided around the world, opportunity is not. Now about 1,800 students in more than 90 countries are participating in our two-year master's program of 14 courses, and enrollment is growing fast. Every seven weeks we begin with a new cohort; the courses run sequentially. More than half of our students are in sub-Saharan Africa – several hundred in Nigeria alone (not surprising given its size) – plus others in Asia, Russia, and across Europe. We're in the process of getting the university accredited; this will take a few years because, among other things, we need graduates. WorldQuant isn't looking to directly benefit through the university, and we don't want students thinking it's a path to a job at the firm. In fact, as a nonprofit we agreed that students cannot be hired at WorldQuant for at least a year. Our goal is to teach these students 21st-century science that they can bring to their communities.

I've asked the university team to begin looking at expanding the curriculum into the data sciences. The group already is launching a data-engineering program, starting with an eight-week "boot camp" in data sciences, much of which involves working with computer programs such as Python. This shorter session could be used as an assessment tool for judging students' capacity for dealing with more advanced material.

One last thing. Today about 90% of WorldQuant University's students are men. That alone suggests great potential for growth, by broadening out the talent pool, which is currently small, to include more women. We are just scratching the surface of reaching talented people all around the world and are committed to providing equal opportunity.

Talent appears to be distributed by a power law. If you take any large sample of people, you'll find that a small fraction of them are particularly good at a given task. The size of this talent pool is simply a matter of statistics. That's why we feel we must reach out to as many countries as possible and avoid any artificial division into groups, based on any kind of artificial criteria. And if we can't get to them physically, we'll use the WebSim platform to reach them across the internet.

In March 2015, I personally paid for everyone in the company, about 700 in all, including some guests, to gather for a meeting at a resort in Puerto Rico. We called it a global summit. By then I was convinced of the power of the exponential revolution that was sweeping quantitative finance. This was a long way from my days as a lone trader at Millennium, wrestling with my one and only alpha. It was even further from Belarus, or New York City, or Wichita. I spoke to the summit about the challenges of operating in a world that was growing exponentially. Data, knowledge, and computing power (driven by Moore's law) were all growing exponentially.

What does it mean to think exponentially? It means continually setting goals. It means understanding that what is shocking today is normal tomorrow and useless the day after. It means thinking and acting with audacity, not complacency; in an exponential world what's here today won't be here tomorrow. It means not believing in limits, which are temporary and exist only to be broken. It means taking risk as a way of life. In an exponential world the terrain we see is always unknown. Turbulence is inevitable. In such unknown terrain there are unknown obstacles and traps, but the rewards for those who can digest all this information also are growing exponentially.

In 2014, the year before our global summit, I'd laid out for the company the fundamental pillars of WorldQuant: Alphas are infinite, talent is global, trading can be taught, and we hold the future of trading in our hands. We had our global alpha factory. Our goal at that time was to produce 1 million alphas, and despite the aggressiveness of that target, we were close to meeting it. And then I tripled that goal. Our constraints were, and are, computer cycles, not ideas. In exponential growth every new goal seems shocking.

Thriving in an exponential world requires boldness and execution. For the Puerto Rico summit, we brought in a handful of American military leaders – former secretary of State Colin Powell, retired general Stanley McChrystal, and retired admiral James Stavridis – to speak to the group. Why? These men understood running organizations in conditions that resembled exponential growth. They understood quick decision making, discipline, risk, and the need to execute at a high level under stress. Of course, quant finance is very different from war. But there's always competition, and it's always right behind you. In an exponential world the enemy never sleeps, the winner takes all, and we always must be one step ahead.

In an exponential world you have to go to war against linear thinking. Exponential thinking involves living with risk. Linear thinking involves certainty, which to me is a kind of death: What in this world is as certain as death? As the world changes exponentially, we have to keep up with it, adjust to it.

Over the years we calculated that the number of alphas we developed appeared to be directly proportional to the number of simulations we ran. You get as many answers as the questions you ask. In fact, our business results tend to be proportional to the logarithm of the number of alphas. We've verified this experimentally. In layman's terms it means that for the business to grow in a linear fashion, the number of alphas must grow exponentially every year. Beneath that math there are always trade-offs among human capital, performance, and productivity. How many people do we hire? How much do we invest? How many ideas do we put into production? Ideas may be infinite, but production is constrained by cost. How do we put the best ideas into production?

WorldQuant exists because of the power of diversity. You can't escape the central UnRule: *All theories and all methods have flaws.*

Nothing can be proved with absolute certainty, but anything can be disproved, and nothing that can be articulated is perfect. But out of this prison of negatives emerges a positive argument for the free exchange of ideas.

> *Value diverse and competing methods.* Because all theories are flawed, the best approach is to collect as many of them as possible and use them all, in as optimal a fashion as you can devise, simultaneously.
>
> *Value multiple, independent points of view.* Smart advisers, each counseling you independently, can dramatically improve the quality of your decisions. Think of each one as an alpha: Five uncorrelated alphas have a very good Sharpe ratio – much better than one.
>
> *Make everyone benefit.* Endeavors that benefit many diverse people have a way of succeeding. Align your endeavor with everyone around you and you will create your own tailwind. That's what I have tried to do at WorldQuant.

CHAPTER 9

Quant Biology

"Think big – it's easier."

By 2013 the exponential growth in data was evident everywhere you looked. The phenomenon had even begun to seep into the popular culture through the markets and the media, captured in the suddenly ubiquitous phrase "Big Data." And following quickly behind Big Data were terms and concepts we had long thought about and worked to master in quantitative investing: predictive algorithms, artificial intelligence, machine learning, and data science. These concepts once seemed to have relatively few applications in the wider world, but that was changing – fast. Starting in 2015, WorldQuant University was building a curriculum around these subjects. Through the WorldQuant Foundation and our venture-investing initiatives, I began to explore these ideas in contexts separate from the trading business.

In the spring of 2014, I had lunch with a very bright young researcher at Weill Cornell Medicine in New York. His name was Dr. Christopher Mason, and he was overseeing a lab focused on developing novel techniques for DNA sequencing, and using algorithms to study the human genome and disease.

We lunched in Weill Cornell's faculty dining room. Mason was an intriguing figure. Then 35, with a Yale Ph.D. in genetics, he enthusiastically bounced from subject to subject, from genomics and DNA sequencing to microbiomes – the microorganisms that live inside and on our bodies – to swabbing techniques designed to pick up bacterial DNA on the New York subway system, part of a project to create a microbial genomic map of the city. An associate professor of physiology and biophysics, Mason also was working with the National Aeronautics and Space Administration to test the effects on DNA and RNA of microgravity and other space-related environmental factors. He told me he was thinking about a 500-year research plan to explore and settle Mars, noting the obvious fact that he wouldn't be around to see its conclusion. After lunch he took me on a tour of his group's wet lab, where many of the samples were sequenced, and the dry lab, where the computational analysis took place.

I found it all fascinating, but in Mason's dry lab – actually, in the dry lab's machine, or computer, room – I began to sense affinities between our two operations. The dry lab looked a lot like WorldQuant, with the same cubicles and computers, many of the same programs, and a similar air of quiet industry and brilliant young talent.

Soon after my visit the WorldQuant Foundation donated $1 million to Weill Cornell to fund an annual $50,000 in-house research scholarship. Since then Mason's group has received three of these scholarships.

Our relationship subsequently expanded beyond a straightforward philanthropic contribution. After that initial lunch Mason and I continued to talk – over dinners, on the phone, in emails. We discussed quantitative finance and predictive biology, and the possibility of modeling disease. He sent me papers and reported on discoveries in his lab. In some ways Mason's lab was a world apart from my firm. Mason and his colleagues were part of a world-renowned medical college, and they were engaged in efforts to understand, predict, and conquer disease, not to extract returns from a relentlessly changing market. Mason was not someone who carefully parceled out his words. His conversation ran like a bubbling stream down a hillside. But we were talking the same language. We were both working to extract signals from extremely complex, nonlinear systems. We were both using computer science to discern patterns in an exploding quantity of data.

Still, as Mason often pointed out to me, the differences between us shouldn't be discounted. At WorldQuant we build many thousands of alphas, which may last for months or years; Mason is focused on developing a handful of models that will help patients plan for 30 or 40 years. As Mason says, the quant paradigm is inverted in medicine. In trading we have learned to live with alphas that last for a short time and then fade. After all, markets change quickly. We can cope with winning, say, 51% of the time. That's really not a good model for health care.

"If you said, 'I'll correctly guess whether your cancer is aggressive or not about 50% of the time,' that would be awful," Mason notes. "Generally, in medicine you have to be right at least 80 to 85% of the time or else people don't take you seriously. You wouldn't want to tell someone, 'Well, you know, you might die or you might not; I'll just go flip a coin.'"

And yet the UnRule applies in both worlds: *No model is a perfect representation of a complex and ever-changing reality.* Every market is different, and so is every patient. Change is a constant. These are huge challenges for Mason and his colleagues.

Eventually, we began to talk about a partnership between quantitative finance and quantitative genomics. What could we learn from each other?

Medicine hasn't always been a source of usable data on disease. Ancient physicians, including Hippocrates and Galen, did try to understand causation in disease, linking ailments to the environment, but theories outpaced hard knowledge. That began to change in the 17th century, when the first quantitative research into the incidence and patterns of disease appeared and the first tools to look more deeply into biology emerged.

Over the next few centuries, the empirical discipline we now know as epidemiology slowly developed. *Epi* is Greek for "upon us" or "among us," and epidemiology is the study of "what is upon the people." Why were there clusters of cholera in London in the 1850s? What could we learn about the propagation of epidemics, such as how they were transmitted? In the 20th century mathematics was introduced into this work, leading to large-scale studies such as those linking lung cancer to smoking, which included conclusions shaped by probability and statistics. By then the agents of disease, such as viruses and bacteria, had been discovered. As in finance, that effort, which still struggled to explain causation, tossed up lots of data.

The study of heredity and what came to be called genes had made a major advance in the 19th century when Austrian monk Gregor Mendel produced his seminal, albeit initially ignored, paper on inheritance and diversity in pea plants. (Mendel's paper was nearly lost, then rediscovered after his death.) The pace accelerated in the 20th century with the exploration of genes and chromosomes, and the discovery of deoxyribonucleic acid, or DNA. The real breakthrough came with the elucidation of the structure of DNA, in 1953, by James Watson and Francis Crick – a finding that suggested a genetic *code*. DNA turned out to be a very long sequential code and, if it could be broken, many believed the key to a vast trove of information.

DNA is made up of a long sequence of a small number of nucleotides – adenine (A), cytosine (C), guanine (G), and thymine (T) – that pair off as rungs in a twisting double-helix ladder packed into every cell: A matches up to T, C with G. In fact, DNA resembles the tape containing instructions for Turing's theoretical computing machine: The biological programming language, in its simplest terms, consists of strings of As and Cs, Ts and Gs. Those sequences direct the cellular machinery through a related nucleic acid, ribonucleic acid, or RNA, which orders the assembly of amino acids into myriad proteins. The DNA code, which resides in the vault of every cellular nucleus, orders up RNA in segments of three base pairs. CAT, for instance, codes for the amino acid histidine. The triplet "system" has a total of 64 possible combinations for only 20 amino acids. Those surplus triplet codes perform other functions, such as starting and stopping what's known as DNA expression. ATG, for example, launches protein production.

Watson and Crick's Nobel Prize-winning work (with crystallographer Maurice Wilkins, who performed some of the original research generating structural images of DNA through X-ray diffraction) led in 1958 to a rule, first postulated by Crick, of molecular biology's "central dogma": DNA provides the essential assembly information that is passed along – "transcripted," or copied – to RNA, which then "translates" it into the cellular production of specific proteins. The central dogma describes an information flow: DNA encodes RNA; RNA encodes proteins. The information moves in one direction only; it cannot flow back from proteins to the genome.

More than half a century later, researchers are still exploring the complexities of that biochemical code. The immensely long genomic sequence of DNA – 3 billion base pairs, 19,000–20,000 protein-coding genes – has presented many mysteries to be solved, from the location and sequence of specific genes to large stretches of noncoding DNA (which make up some 98% of the total genome) to processes such as RNA splicing or gene transposition (in which genes suddenly change chromosomal positions). In 1960 molecular biologists discovered two kinds of RNA: messenger RNA and transfer RNA.

The first genome to be completely sequenced, an influenza microbe, was released in 1995; the Human Genome Project published the first draft of the entire human genome in 2000 and the completed version in 2004. Throughout, the pattern has been much the same. Fundamental breakthroughs like the elucidation of DNA or the sequencing of the genome generate enthusiasm, particularly in the public (and the markets), only to reveal ever-deepening complexity; an answer elicits many more questions. It turns out that the central dogma itself is another example of the UnRule: While it applies broadly, we now know there are many exceptions to it. Those exceptions have led to important new avenues of investigation.

Meanwhile, the technological tools have been improving in spectacular fashion, making exponential leaps in performance. High-throughput genomic sequencing alone is racing forward at a rate that evokes Moore's law. The Human Genome Project spent about $3 billion over 13 years to sequence the entire human genome; Mason notes that since 2006 the cost of sequencing a genome has been halved every five months. One company, Solexa, which was acquired by San Diego-based Illumina in 2007, announced it had reduced the cost of sequencing a human genome to $1,000 by 2016, with a plan to get to $100 by 2020.

A consequence of the rapid advances in sequencing is that genomic data is growing at an exponential rate. Today there are many dozens of databases that researchers can use to submit or access genomic data. Large and growing datasets such as the Encyclopedia of DNA Elements, housed at the international ENCODE Consortium, are assembling a comprehensive list of functional elements in the human genome. The Cancer Genome Atlas, or TCGA, a part of the National Cancer Institute and the National Human Genome Research Institute, is mapping genetic changes in 33 different cancers. The International Cancer Genome Consortium is working to generate comprehensive genomic data on some 50 cancers. Mason's lab runs its own high-throughput sequencing to develop cell-specific molecular maps that attempt to provide a multidimensional view of disease at the cellular level.

What we're discovering, step by step, is how nature, through evolution, has spun the web of life at the molecular and atomic levels. We all share the great bulk of sequences, but there are a surprising number of variations in individual genomes, some of which are passed down to later generations. These mutations and transpositions, caused by everything from environmental damage to mistakes made during replication, may spawn diseases or chronic conditions, or they may ensure good health and drive the evolution of the species, providing the mechanism for Darwinian evolution through natural selection.

Mason and his colleagues often liken the central dogma to looking for your keys beneath a lamppost even though you know you lost them elsewhere. Mason compares it to astronomy in the 17th century, when our view of the cosmos was limited to a few crude instruments that could magnify only the thin slice of the electromagnetic spectrum known as visible light.

In both astronomy and biology, we have wandered far from the lamppost. The father of genomics was Frederick Sanger, a British biochemist who in the 1950s painstakingly determined the amino acid sequence of the protein insulin; this involved about a kilobyte of data. Sanger went on to sequence the more complex RNA in the 1960s and some nucleotide sequences of DNA in the 1970s, work that entailed hundreds of kilobytes of data. He won two Nobel Prizes in chemistry for his work. A few years later molecular biologists realized that sequencing a complete human genome, like working out the structure of DNA, was a beginning as much as an end. Today modern sequencing machines in labs like Mason's generate hundreds of terabytes of data *every day*.

Disciplines such as proteomics, the large-scale study of proteins; bioinformatics, the development of software tools to analyze biological data; and computational biology, the process of analyzing and interpreting that data, have fully emerged. Research into notoriously difficult diseases like Alzheimer's or many forms of cancer has taken on new life. Mason himself works in areas that were pretty much unknown a generation ago but which embody the shifting, cross-fertilizing landscape of modern biomedicine, molecular biology, and bioinformatics: metagenomics, computational genomics, and predictive biology.

Consider one research area Mason and his colleagues have pursued over the past few years. Like DNA, RNA consists of four bases, but it has one variation, with uracil replacing thymine. There are more than 100 known modifications or markers that occur within RNA, modulating its activities in various ways – regulating it. One of the most common of these markers is the so-called methyl group, a small molecule of one carbon atom and three hydrogen atoms that attaches itself to RNA or DNA through the mediation of specific enzymes. One of these modifications, the m6A-methyl-adenosine, occurs at some 12,000 locations on 7,000 genes, mostly at the endpoints of individual genes, and is usually associated with the role of turning them on or off. M6A markers appear to have important regulatory functions. Moreover, these RNA modifications may affect DNA modifications; the m6A appears to be a negative regulator of RNA editing, in which some cells can make changes in sequences after transcription. But m6A is just a single marker – one signal – in a vast and only partly explored thicket rich with signals, some strong, others much more ambiguous. In fact, there are layers of regulators in this system, which like the markets include multiple feedback loops and interactions.

As Mason notes, Crick's central dogma has broken down. DNA can replicate itself; RNA can act in both directions (that is, in protein assembly or on DNA); proteins in turn can modify RNA. There are about 100 million gigabytes of data in the entire human genome. But that doesn't include the activities of multiple regulatory levels – the epigenome (DNA), the epitranscriptome (RNA), the epiproteome (proteins) – that interact in ways researchers are still sorting out, or the collection of all the proteins produced in the body, known as the proteome, or the teeming universe of microbes in and on the organism, the microbiome, all of which may play some role, good, bad, or unknown, in the living organism. In Mason's words, "It's complex."

And we still have much to learn. When you aggregate all the factors in the environment that can affect the machinery of DNA, RNA, and proteins, as well as account for changes that occur over time, Mason estimates you would need to store 1 trillion terabytes of data – that is, 1,000 to the eighth power, or a yottabyte – to get a complete data picture of human biology. We can't do that today, but that's where all this is heading.

When Mason and I first spoke, he said, "I want to be able to predict everything about anything." That got my attention – that was thinking *really* big – though he admitted his goal might be a little aggressive; it reminded me of my own out-there targets for alphas. Prediction, he stressed, was embedded within every project in his labs at Weill Cornell.

He explained to me: "What I mean is that for medicine, for most of biology, we often don't know the most informative place to look. Where and what kind of molecular signatures are the most indicative for health or disease are still being discovered. So when I say we want to predict everything about anything, it means I want to construct frameworks that can leverage as much as possible to build a better view of cancer evolution, of how we understand infectious disease."

The PathoMap, Mason's project to map the microbes, viruses, and potential pathogens and their genomes in the New York subway, revealed all kinds of eye-catching data about a widely trafficked part of the city, including the fact that 48% of the microbes detected were essentially unknown. These details fascinated the media. As Mason told *The New York Times*, the subway system, with its 5.5 million daily riders, was a "rain forest" to explore. Mason's PathoMap, the first of similar initiatives, known as MetaSUB, in major cities around the globe, illuminated the world of the microbiome, which long ago in evolutionary history took up a symbiotic residence in the human body, though few humans realize it exists. In fact, we each carry around about 100 trillion bacteria, weighing three to five pounds, and leave traces of them on everything from subway poles and turnstiles to doorknobs and telephones. Mason has a number of one-liners he uses about the microbiome, including "In your body's cellular democracy, you are a minority party" and "Most of the genes in your body are not yours."

He emphasizes how important the microbiome is to the health of the body's ecosystem, and the consequences of losing that diversity. "Microbiome" refers not only to the mass of bacteria but also to the genes they contain – 100 times more than the human genome. These bacterial genes produce proteins essential for digestion, nutrition, immune health, and the regulation of appetite and weight gain. Bacteria in the body produce about 700 "drugs," including 90% of the body's serotonin and 50% of its dopamine, not to say key vitamins. The occasional pathogen also appears.

(The human genome may be in a vault, but it's hardly locked away. Some 98,000 viruses have left their DNA in the human genome since we broke off from the chimpanzees. And 300 genes from the mitochondria, the machinery in the cell that produces chemical energy, also reside in the genome. Mitochondria genomes bear some resemblance to those of microbes.)

The PathoMap study had a more serious, long-term goal than learning what subway stations had the most exotic bacteria. It was designed to establish an analytical baseline in which repeated sampling could be used to assess long-term disease surveillance, incidents of bioterrorism, and large-scale health management. That is, it was designed to be predictive in a number of different ways.

There are signals in all those sequenced genomes, whether from subway-dwelling microbes or from the scrambled genomes of patients undergoing cancer treatment. Mason believes we have come to the point where we can begin to monitor and sequence individual human cells and the communication among cells. We can examine every mutation in any cancer cell through rapid and cost-effective sequencing. He sees two challenges ahead. First, technologically, how can we capture and correctly profile individual cells or individual molecules from patients? Second, how do we model changes in, say, an elusive, persistent, heterogenous disease like cancer? Can you read the DNA sequence in a way that tells you something actionable about the future?

"When you sequence a piece of DNA, how much can it tell you forensically about where it comes from in the world and what potential risk or signal it can provide for medicine?" Mason asks. "From our perspective, we want to look at a sequence of DNA that comes from a particular cell in the body and understand everything we possibly can about it. What does it mean for your risk for disease based on the mutational state of it? What does it indicate about health? What drugs will work? To answer these questions, you'll need Big Data and better technology."

Mason and I have discussed whether I could ever imagine a financial model that would be good and last 30 years, which of course is impossible to do. But it's what's essential in predictive medicine in that you need to say, "Okay, given your genome at age 15 or 18, here is whether or not you should have a prophylactic bilateral mastectomy. If you have a BRCA1 mutation, you have to decide whether you would literally remove parts of your body to save the rest." That's a decision that can only be made considering a lifelong time frame.

As Mason and I continued our conversations, we began talking about what it would take to more effectively model diseases. Unsurprisingly, money led the list. Cash would allow him to hire more researchers and buy more of the sophisticated hardware required to look into individual cells and do more rapid sequencing and complex analysis of cancer cells. But we also saw an opportunity to cross-fertilize our operations. It's true that WorldQuant's goal was different from Mason's and our models were very different. However, we both employed lots of Ph.D.s, computer scientists, and IT professionals; we engaged in research; and we fed off data. We used many of the same programming languages and spoke a similar math and science language; we shared a quantitative mind-set. At WorldQuant we knew how to quickly introduce our scientifically trained recruits to finance. What if we dropped a few of our researchers onto Mason's planet and brought some of his grad students and postdocs to our offices? Call it an experiment that would attempt to blend quant finance and quant genomics to improve the techniques used in both worlds.

And that's what we've done. In the spring of 2017, WorldQuant deepened its collaboration by donating $5 million to establish the WorldQuant Initiative for Quantitative Prediction at Weill Cornell, which, Mason told me, would be "the first initiative that blends Big Data in cancer biology with the microbiome, and Big Data in what's called metagenomics, or all the genomes, both human and microbial." Mason and Weill Cornell associate professor Olivier Elemento, who is applying Big Data to understanding why drugs fail in clinical trials, will oversee the research initiative, housed in the Institute for Computational Biomedicine at Weill Cornell. That effort will work with scientists at Weill Cornell's Caryl and Israel Englander Institute for Precision Medicine and the Sandra and Edward Meyer Cancer Center.

We've agreed that Mason's lab will take a handful of WorldQuant researchers, adept at the use of predictive algorithms, as visiting fellows. They'll serve as data scientists whose mission is to immerse themselves in the genomic datasets and come up with new ideas. Mason will send some of his people to WorldQuant to learn some of the approaches we take to data.

As I write this, the program has just begun. We've sent several WorldQuanters to Weill Cornell; Mason's folks have just been chosen and are about to join us at WorldQuant. We're hoping that by combining some of the best minds, algorithms, and methods of our two organizations we'll get a better understanding of how to prevent and treat disease and at the same time improve our alpha research techniques. This is the first experiment of its kind, and we're both excited and hopeful.

What are Mason and his colleagues searching for in that enormous haystack of genomic data? Essentially, they want to pinpoint correspondences between genomic sequences and genetic diseases – the kind of relations that predictive algorithms can be constructed around. In biological jargon the genotype (the genomic sequence) often finds its reflection in the phenotype (the physical manifestations). Form determines function.

Some of these correspondences have been established already. There is a growing list of diseases, such as hemophilia, caused by a defective gene that impairs blood clotting, and sickle-cell anemia, triggered by a single base-pair mutation in one amino acid. We know that a mutation in the so-called CFTR gene impairs the transport of chloride ions and water across cell membranes, resulting in the condition known as cystic fibrosis. We know that some breast and ovarian cancers are associated with inherited mutations in the BRCA1 gene and that Huntington's disease is caused by a mutation in a gene (a stretch of the triplet CAG that's repeated 50 or 60 times), which produces a large, attenuated protein that accumulates in and damages brain cells. But while the list is fairly long and growing, the number of known genetic mutations is tiny compared with the very large number of protein interactions that occur.

It is difficult to construct algorithms that can anticipate diseases traced to multiple genes, cascades of genes, or multiple mutations (caused by environmental damage or replication mistakes) or obscure feedback loops. We know more and more, but the rain forest remains vast and complex, with many regions of the map still blank. However, the rapidly growing knowledge base provides targets for algorithms, some of which, like WorldQuant alphas, may prove to be effective.

The accelerating advances in molecular biology and genomics toss up some serious ethical and political challenges. How safe is all this? Who owns this information? How far should genomic manipulation go? What we have learned about genes and genomes presents Mason and his colleagues with both a challenge and an opportunity: Health is personal, and not just in the sense that it's *your* health. There is a surprisingly large amount of variation and adaptation in individual human genomes, much of which seems to have no obvious phenotypic effect. We are quite different from one another. A mutation may or may not cause cancer. A drug may work effectively, a little bit, or not at all. A pack-a-day smoker may live to 110. A serious vegan may die of a heart attack.

The more we learn, the more complicated the genome appears. Sequencing has shown that individual genomes may contain repeated portions of entire genes, and transposable elements that jump around. Given the necessary precision of human development and neurophysiology, the genome had to possess either large functional redundancies – backup systems like the engines on Lorange's North Sea ship – or very few critical genetic structures that could break down. Mason leans toward the former. That diversity and variation help explain why the one-size-fits-all of most current therapies often fails, goes awry, or produces side effects.

It also explains why truly personalized medicine, driven by fast and inexpensive sequencing, remains a touchstone for researchers like Mason. Sequencing provides access to the individual genome; the $1,000-heading-toward-$100 genome is a force for medical democratization. Computers and algorithms can quickly detect patterns and identify trends into the future. Already there are genetic markers that indicate individual responses to certain drugs; the application of the marriage of pharmacology and genomics, a field known as pharmacogenomics, promises greater effectiveness and precision.

While precision medicine is still developing, there is an opportunity for it to advance beyond its current state. It points the way toward a time not too far off when medical care can be intensely data-driven, customized, and predictive.

CHAPTER 10

The Age of Prediction

"Quantity is quality."

I n the 1940s, Viennese theoretical physicist Erwin Schrödinger was living and working in Dublin. Like many of his colleagues, he had fled Central Europe with the rise of the Nazis and impending war. Schrödinger, whose father was a chemist and amateur botanist, had long been fascinated by biology, particularly by the advances that were being made in heredity and genetics. In a series of lectures in 1943, Schrödinger crossed another boundary, taking the approach of quantum mechanics and applying it to biology, describing the molecular nature of life from a purely theoretical knowledge of physics. This became a legendary book titled *What Is Life?*

Schrödinger's lectures had an enormous effect. His ideas not only inspired physicists to tackle the molecular basis of life – and anticipated and encouraged the emergence of molecular biology – they accurately predicted the physical nature of DNA, which at that moment was being isolated and identified as a nucleic acid by Oswald Avery in New York.

The Viennese physicist began with a simple question: "How can the events *in space and time* which take place within the spatial boundaries of a living organism be accounted for by physics and chemistry?" Matters of heredity and inheritance had to be, he said, fundamentally atomic and molecular. As a result, physicists understood that "all the physical and chemical laws that are known to play an important part in the life of organisms are of this statistical kind."

Schrödinger noted the paradox we have touched on in its various manifestations: the emergence of some form of order in nature arising from a deep Brownian disorder – as he put it, the "unceasing heat motion of the atoms." Then he made a breathtaking leap: The chromosome fiber *had* to consist of what he called an aperiodic crystal – that is, a long, linear crystal in which the units are not identical. Ordinary periodic crystals, with repeating faces and lattices, "are very interesting and complicated objects," he said, but compared with aperiodic crystals, "they are rather plain or dull. The difference in structure is of the same kind as that between an ordinary wallpaper in which the same pattern is repeated again and again in regular periodicity and a masterpiece of embroidery, say a Raphael tapestry, which shows no dull repetition, but an elaborate, coherent, meaningful design traced by a great master."

These aperiodic crystals were, in Schrödinger's opinion, "the material carrier of life."

He went on to describe a molecule full of contradictory traits. It had to possess chemical regularity to copy and transmit information, but it had to be irregular as well to accommodate the kind of change and diversity we see in nature. It had to contain an enormous amount of information yet fit into a microscopic cell. He imagined it stretched out in strands of chromosomes, which already had been identified as the genetic material. And he guessed that it contained a "variety of contents compressed in the miniature code."

Nature is nonlinear and complex. Nature is a constant struggle between order and randomness, between signal and noise. Von Neumann, Ulam, Schrödinger, Turing, Bachelier, Black, Sornette, Mandelbrot, and many others struggled to define, often mathematically, some aspect of that underlying order, which is statistical and often spookily paradoxical, from the turbulent flow of neutrons to the random walk of markets.

A code, no matter how difficult or miniature, is a kind of order; what we do at WorldQuant and Chris Mason does at Weill Cornell is *decode*. Today, using powerful computers, sophisticated software, and a lot of diverse data, many groups in many disciplines are trying to discern often faint signals in complex, nonlinear systems: the markets; the weather; the physical universe, from subatomic particles to the cosmos to biology and life itself. The key to finding these islands of order is information. What Schrödinger calls the material of life and we now call genomics is fundamentally a code that can be broken, as Turing did with the Enigma machine. It provides at least the potential for predictability where once none seemed to exist.

∽

In *What Is Life?* Schrödinger presented himself as developing "a naive physicist's ideas about organisms," and he asked what he admitted was "an odd, almost ludicrous question: Why are atoms so small?" In fact, he was reaching for a profound point about not just biology but the physical universe. Atoms are small and exist in such large numbers because they are individually always in a state of disorder, except at absolute zero, when they cease moving entirely. It's a variation on the law of large numbers. Imagine, he says, how difficult it would be to think if our senses were susceptible to the actions of a single atom or molecule. But while the behavior of individual atoms – bouncing randomly, like rubber balls and stock prices – is disordered, physicists can predict the behavior of large numbers of atoms with great precision. Scale matters. Atoms are small, as Schrödinger noted, because organisms (even viruses and microbes) are large.

For a number of years at Millennium and WorldQuant, and across the quantitative financial industry, we debated among ourselves the question of quality versus quantity when it came to alphas. Would it be better to produce only a handful of extremely powerful alphas that could last a long time but pose an existential threat to the firm when they failed, or to develop many alphas that could respond to fainter signals and might not last as long but would allow us to continually monitor, rethink, and readjust our portfolios?

A number of quant shops took the first path, but I'd always leaned toward quantity. I could never satisfactorily define what quality was, and after a while the debate felt like it would never end. For a time we at WorldQuant had no idea whether we would even be able to construct algorithms in large numbers to detect weaker signals. Eventually, though, I came to the realization that the second path was not only possible but more effective for us over the long term. It's the atomic paradox: Individual atoms behave in random ways, but in bulk – and this means a very large number – they begin to behave in ways that are quantifiable and predictable.

Still, at WorldQuant we continued to debate this question. For every idea there was a counter-idea, and we never got anywhere; whenever we tried to generate what we thought were "quality" alphas, we failed. In the end I came to believe that the quality argument required a kind of faith. To my mind quantity *was* quality. If you took 1,000 signals that would last a long time, that was quality.

As we added more and more alphas, people warned that they'd stop working, but we pushed past those limits. There turned out to be no limit. Similarly, there seems to be no limit on people who say there's a limit.

So we concluded that, in our opinion, quantity is far superior to quality (though some quants will undoubtedly disagree). It came down to something very concrete, particularly to a quant like myself: You could define quantity – count the alphas – but not quality. And that finally ended the debate at WorldQuant.

Quantity is also important when it comes to data. Alphas generate valuable information; the growth of alphas and the quantity of data we can access go hand in hand. Generally, the quantity and diversity of financial data, or data that has financial or investment implications, have grown exponentially and will continue to grow as the world becomes more automated and interconnected. The exponential growth in the number of alphas at WorldQuant is representative of the much larger trend.

Clearly, we have been in the Age of Big Data for a number of years. In 2012 the World Economic Forum published a report titled "Big Data, Big Impact: New Possibilities for International Development." The report said that in 2012 the world was giving birth to more than 2.5 quintillion bytes of data every day, poured forth by everything from satellites and social media to credit cards and smartphones. That number is much larger today. The report also noted that the mobile data traffic just from emerging countries was expected to grow 100% annually through 2015. A quintillion, by the way, is a billion billion, or 1 followed by 18 zeroes: 1,000,000,000,000,000,000. Research firm IDC forecasts that the total volume of data will grow from 44 zettabytes in 2020 to 180 zettabytes by 2025. A zettabyte is a 1 followed by 21 zeroes. That's a huge number, but it's smaller than Mason's yottabyte, the total amount of potential data in the human organism, a 1 followed by 24 zeroes.

The WEF report emphasized the changes wrought by a single technology, the mobile phone, ticking off novel uses of suddenly accessible data from around the world: the health researchers in

San Francisco who can quantify a disease outbreak taking place on the far side of the globe by analyzing cell phone data; the United Nations aid agency that can detect signs of drought in the Sahara from mobile data. "Much attention is paid to the vital services that mobile phone technology has brought to billions of people in the developing world," the report noted. "But now many policy-makers, corporate leaders and development experts are realising the potential applications ... for the enormous amounts of data created *by and about* the individuals who use these services."

Today an interconnected world of cell phone users seems like yesterday's news. Now experts are predicting a new, potentially even larger wave of data arising from the Internet of Things (IoT), the rapidly growing use of computing devices embedded in ordinary appliances and tools and connected across the internet, often accessed through the burgeoning universe of smartphone apps. That wave will challenge the current IT infrastructure, propelling software development to manage and analyze it, further driving the fast-growing cloud vendors to provide enough data storage and producing jobs in data management and analytics. It also should generate many signals for WorldQuant alphas. The IoT can include everything from the daily data from personal health devices, vehicles, appliances, thermostats, and security systems to "smart" energy grids and wired cities to ubiquitous video cameras live-streaming everything from elk migrations to terrorist hot spots. And we're just at the start.

But I'm convinced that the Age of Big Data has if not passed then already been normalized for many people, as quickly as it arrived. We have begun to take it for granted. Still, it's one thing to possess a great amount of data; it's another thing entirely to make it useful – to make it accessible, digestible, and *predictive*. I believe that has begun to occur, and that we'll be at this for a very long time.

We've now entered the Age of Prediction. For everything we're trying to predict – securities prices, retail sales, unemployment, weather, health, security in a variety of guises – the amount of data is growing exponentially. The good news: By following certain mathematical laws, you should get a linear increase in predictability as long as the data continues to grow at a nonlinear rate. If all things hold constant, everything will become more and more predictable from the perspective of the data. In fact, the Age of Prediction is not some wacky, far-off idea; it's already having major effects, though we may not always recognize it. For companies it's improving manufacturing and marketing efficiencies. At WorldQuant it's enhancing our ability to deliver quality returns to investors. For predictive medicine, like the research initiative we've launched with Chris Mason at Weill Cornell, it holds the promise of extending or saving lives.

Technology is critical for success in the Age of Prediction. Organizations that can effectively employ machine learning and artificial intelligence to analyze and exploit all this data will have an advantage over their less technically sophisticated peers. But machines are not taking over like in some science-fiction thriller, as many fear. People will remain essential and vital to this process, if they are trained in the kinds of technical, quantitative disciplines that WorldQuant University offers. You need lots of people with lots of different ideas and opinions because the key to better prediction is combining many different models. Once you have the right people, you need the ability to test quickly and easily. Here simulation technology plays a key role. Machine learning and AI can help develop more models, amplifying the role of the people at the center of the process. Instead of producing one model, a human aided by technology can produce thousands of them.

We have not arrived at utopia. And if the UnRule is still valid in the future, we may never do so. The bad news: Technology, connectivity, and complexity trigger powerful countervailing forces, like the fractures in Sornette's Kevlar pressure tanks or the volatility in a peaking market. The exponential growth in data is making the world increasingly complex as the frequency of events accelerates and the world grows more chaotic geopolitically. A host of issues triggers insecurities, anxieties, and political reaction: privacy, control, a deepening divide between those who can flourish in this interconnected, data-rich world and those who struggle. Transportation is swift, communications instantaneous. Even as some organizations are able to predict events with greater accuracy, everything is getting more complicated. And if you can't predict things more accurately, that complexity could easily overwhelm you – as an individual, a CEO, or even a national leader.

We all have our philosophies, whether we know it or not. We've all been formed by some combination of experience and thought. Looking back on my life – Belarus, my journey to the United States, the powerful influence my parents had on me; my odyssey through video gaming, computer science, and finance; my work at Bell Labs, Timber Hill, Millennium, and WorldQuant – it's easy to construct a simple story that fits snugly together. All the facts are there, all the context. We know how the story ends, at least for now.

But we don't live backwards. Even in the Age of Prediction, we often lack the data required to truly know what the future holds. There's a tension between our increasing ability to use data to predict and the fact that we may never have enough to fully capture a fluid, shape-shifting reality. My mind was shaped by a series of challenges in which the future nearly always was uncertain and decisions had to be made based on too little data. I was bright enough to deal with complex problems fairly early on: chess, math, computer science – endeavors that are difficult because often there aren't easy answers.

My parents plunged into the unknown when they opted for freedom. I took the Millennium job almost randomly, not really knowing much more than I liked Izzy. In the 2007 quant quake, I had to make decisions, first to get out of the market, then to get back in, based on experience and intuition. Quants are supposed to *know*, which is crazy.

Predicting the future remains a challenging and humbling endeavor.

Over the years I have learned a lot of math, programming, and finance, and I remain convinced that only the empirical approach makes sense. As a result, I install testing and simulation at the core of our alpha production process. Many of the rules I've developed over the years deal directly with the demands of the empirical approach – that is, to experiment using the best information available, to test and retest but be ready to cut losses, rethink positions, and move in another direction if the strategy is not working out. All of these require you to keep your ego out of your decisions.

The UnRule is a testament to the fact that the more you look deeply into both physical and social systems, the more obvious it is how strange reality is – spooky strange. You can only guess why things work the way they do. Why are there power laws, or fractal mirror images as you scale? Empiricism is the natural strategy for the UnRule. Does A predict B? If it does, good. If it doesn't, too bad – let's try again. Nothing lasts forever; Gödel revealed that even something as seemingly fundamental as arithmetic cannot be fully proved. As life becomes more and more complicated, there's more and more value in having rules that provide some discipline and order to counter that uncertainty.

More alphas are better because the more you have, the more effectively you can describe reality. It's not describable in any single equation or algorithm. One thousand alphas will describe reality better than one, but 100 million will do a better job than 1,000, and 1 billion will do a better job yet. You see the improvements as you get more signals. That realization helped shape my larger approach.

Value diverse and competing methods. Because all theories are flawed, your best approach is to collect as many of them as possible and use them all simultaneously, in as optimal a way as possible, simultaneously. Similarly, *value multiple independent points of view.* Very smart advisers, each advising you independently, can dramatically improve the quality of your decisions. Think of each one as an alpha: Several good, uncorrelated alphas have a very good Sharpe ratio, much better than any single one.

Basically, the more alphas you have, the more you can make use of weaker and weaker information. There are more weak signals than strong signals, and as strong signals get arbitraged away, they're replaced by lots of weaker signals. This can be explained using the powerful and always seductive metaphor of market efficiency. Once upon a time, there were less efficient markets, when there were only a relatively few strong signals. If you take these thousands or millions of signals, you get something that works just as well as the few signals that once existed. It's much more complicated to orchestrate many weaker signals, but it works.

The quant quake may well have marked the decline of that era of a few strong signals, whether you believe it was caused by a crowded trade, arbitrage, or a systemic failure tied to mortgages. Could it happen again? Nothing ever happens the same way twice. Something will happen, but it will be different. The best defense against destructive drawdowns is to have as many alphas as possible – to be diversified. And that may capture how the efficient market works. First, you get big inefficiencies, then they get destroyed and you're left with many small inefficiencies – signals. But inefficiencies never go away. Someone has to make markets more efficient, and in doing so they'll make money. If they don't do it, someone else will.

I left my homeland at a young age. My experience was hardly unique; thousands fled the Soviet Union in those years, just as in the mid-20th century so many of the leading lights of European math and science experienced departure, resettlement, and exile, and many millions then and today fled and are fleeing terror, war, persecution, natural disasters, or a lack of opportunity (the last a powerful incentive in a connected world). But crossing borders, learning new ways, new languages, and new habits can broaden your perspective. It may make you an empiricist, tolerant of ambiguity and sensitive to paradox – or it may not.

WorldQuant is based in suburban Old Greenwich, but the company is truly global, taking advantage of talent and skills nurtured in dozens of foreign countries. The world often does seem to be disordered; randomly staggering into the future; searching for lost keys under a lamppost, to use Mason's metaphor, while knowing full well that they're somewhere out there in the dark. But in this world the methods of the quantitative sciences provide some semblance of order. Quantitative methods will not resolve the fundamental questions of the universe, ensure our happiness, or whisk us all to heaven. But they are a powerful tool for illuminating processes we have come to realize are far more complex than we once thought, and far more fascinating, and – with time, computing power, and data – far more predictive.

As we make that journey into the future, it behooves us to remember the UnRule: *All theories and all methods have flaws.* Nothing can be proved with absolute certainty, but anything can be disproved, and nothing that can be articulated can be perfect.

That seems to me to be the world we live in. I'm convinced that the Age of Prediction is upon us. But part of the predictive mind-set, which increasingly is essential to effectively compete, is to understand that change is always lurking, even with all the quantitative tools and data we can pull together. It's important not to fall in love with your strategies and to keep your ego in check. More is always better because quantity provides options. But there are no final answers. There is only the paradox of the UnRule.

Index